D1180771

Nelson

Nelson

VICTORIA CAROLAN

POCKET ESSENTIALS

This edition published in 2005 by Pocket Essentials
P.O.Box 394, Harpenden, Herts, AL5 1XJ
www.pocketessentials.com

Distributed in the USA by Trafalgar Square Publishing,
P.O. Box 257, Howe Hill Road, North Pomfret, Vermont 05053

A CIP catalogue record for this book is available from the British Library

ISBN 1 904048 54 4

2 4 6 8 10 9 7 5 3 1

Typeset by Avocet Typeset, Chilton, Aylesbury, Bucks
Printed and bound in Great Britain by Creative Print & Design (Wales)

This book is dedicated to my parents, Michael John Carolan and Valerie Carolan with love and thanks.

Acknowledgements

I would like to offer my thanks to Sean Martin for his support throughout this project, for reading through chapters in the middle of the night and sending me copious notes! Many thanks to my sister Philippa Carolan for her encouragement and belief in me.

I would also like to mention the following people who are not directly responsible for helping me in the writing of this book but without whom I would never have got to this point. Lucy Smith who was the one always telling me to 'give up the day job.'

Professor Sarah Palmer and Professor Roger Knight, my tutors at the Greenwich Maritime Institute who tried to shape me into a decent maritime historian – whatever faults there are in the following book are my own and no reflection on their excellent teaching!

My thanks also to my erstwhile fellow students at Greenwich especially Chris Ware, for his encyclopaedic knowledge of all things maritime (and much else besides) and his unfailing good humour, and Richard Bateman for his unstinting support, quiet diplomacy, and many a bottle of red wine!

Contents

Author's note

This book is intended primarily as an introduction to Nelson, to give a concise history of his life and legacy and to provide pointers towards newly discovered material and other sources for further study.

New material is being discovered about Nelson all the time and this book aims to be as accurate as possible in using the information that is currently available. Where I have found minor discrepancies in details of his life I have pointed them out to the reader or chosen the version that appears to make the most sense.

Nelson's Early Life

Burnham Thorpe

When Horatio Nelson was born on 29 September 1758 there was little to indicate that he was destined to be the most famous admiral that Britain has ever known. He was the third surviving son of Edmund Nelson, the rector of Burnham Thorpe, in Norfolk. Edmund was himself the son of a rector and, while he was by no means poor (he was able to keep four servants), he was neither rich nor a member of the gentry. Nelson's mother, Catherine Sucking, however, did have some illustrious connections and, more importantly for young Horatio, a brother who had distinguished himself in the Royal Navy.

Catherine was daughter of Dr Suckling, the Prebendary of Westminster, and her grandmother was the sister of Sir Robert Walpole, the prime minister to both George I and George II. Nelson's family was not considered of a high enough social position to be invited to Houghton Hall, the nearby seat of the Walpoles: however, from time to time, the Nelsons received a gift of a brace of pheasants from the estate.

At the time of Horatio's birth, Catherine Nelson's brother, Captain Maurice Suckling, was fighting the French in the Caribbean, and had become something of a family hero.

Little is known for sure about Nelson's childhood, and he does not appear in his father's records of the family history until he joined the Navy at the age of 12. There are, however, various tales that may or may not be true that have often been repeated in accounts of his life. Most of these stories come from a book, written in the year after Nelson's death, by James Stainer Clarke and John McArthur. The biography contained many inaccuracies, most of which can be traced back to Nelson's brother William who wanted to present an unblemished account of his sibling. It is illustrated with various tales of Nelson's childhood which are chosen to show that heroism and compassion were evident in his character even when he was a small boy. For example, it is reported that Nelson once became lost while out looking for birds' nests. His grandmother was worried that he had been carried off by gypsies and, when he found his way back, she said to him 'I wonder that fear did not drive you home'. Young Nelson replied: 'I never saw fear. What is it? It never came near me'.

In a similar vein is the tale of Horatio and William trying to get the coach to school after heavy snow and returning home to say that they could not get through.

Their father sent them out again, telling them not to return until they had made quite sure that it was impossible to get to the school. When William decided that, indeed, it was impossible, Horatio disagreed, saying 'Remember, brother, it was left to our honour'. Whether these are myths or not, there is a ring of truth in them when one considers his adult devotion to duty and honour, and his tendency towards arrogance and confidence in his own ability. Certainly his family regarded him as a boy of spirit.

The most traumatic event of Nelson's childhood was the death of his mother in 1767, when he was just nine years old. He later said that 'the thought of former days brings all my mother to my heart, which shows itself in my eyes'. Her influence on Nelson was clearly a strong one. It was known that she had a patriotic and vehement dislike of the French and held naval officers, like her brother Maurice, in great esteem. Nelson was the only one of her sons to join the navy, although he was later to take one of his brothers to sea with him as a ship's chaplain.

After his mother's death, Nelson left the Royal Grammar school in Norwich where he boarded during the term time and was sent first to Downham Market and then to Sir William Paston's School in North Walsham. When Horatio returned home for the Christmas vacation in 1770 with his brother William, they discovered that their father had gone to stay in

Bath to take the waters. At the same time their uncle, Maurice Suckling, had been given command of the 64 gun ship *Raisonnable*. The ship was being fitted out at Chatham as part of the mobilisation to defend the Falkland Islands from Spanish claims. As soon as he knew this, Nelson wanted to join his uncle at sea, and according to his brother William, Nelson asked him to write to their father to request that Suckling took him onto the ship. Captain Suckling gave the now famous reply:

'What has poor Horace done, who is so weak that he, above all the rest, should be sent to rough it at sea? But let him come and the first time we go into action a cannon-ball may knock off his head and provide for him at once.'

This was the decision that would dictate the rest of Nelson's life.

Joining the Navy

Nelson lived through a period of revolutionary change throughout the world, which, in turn, would change the patterns of war. First came the American Revolution (1775-83) with the revolt of the British North American colonies, caused by their opposition to British economic exploitation and their objection to paying for a standing army. Next was the French Revolution (1789-99) which would pave the way for

Napoleon's bid to conquer Europe and the Napoleonic Wars. These were the two principal events that would provide the backdrop for Nelson's career. He was also joining the Navy at a time when it was one of the most successful military forces the world has ever witnessed. Since the navy was the island nation's principal form of defence, it had enormous support from both the government and the commercial sector. As it also protected merchant shipping it was in everyone's interest to keep the navy strong. In 1763 the Seven Years War (a conflict over colonial supremacy) culminated in Britain and Prussia defeating France, Spain, Austria and Russia. Britain took control of India and many colonies previously governed by France. Both France and Spain suffered humiliating defeats and spent the following years re-building their naval forces and looking for opportunities to take their revenge. This was the reason France entered the American War of Independence on the side of the rebels, seeing the possibility of weakening British power. The later Revolutionary Wars with Napoleon saw the French and Spanish fleets built up to such an extent that their combined strength exceeded that of the British Navy. This was what Nelson and his colleagues were to face throughout these years.

So Nelson arrived in Chatham in March 1771 at 12 years old, having to find his own way to the *Raisonnable*. It was not unusual for a 12-year-old boy to go to sea. In fact, some joined the navy as early as seven. Their schooling would be continued in service, with lessons directly relevant to the profession, such as mathematics for the purposes of navigation. Coincidentally, when Nelson reached Chatham, *Victory*, the ship that he would command at Trafalgar, was in dock under repair. There was no welcome because his Uncle was away and the boy was not expected. The weather was windy and it was snowing — not an auspicious beginning to his career. He was assigned a berth in the orlop deck, dark and below the waterline. Even a boy who had never known fear must nevertheless have questioned his resolve for a career in the Navy that first day.

Nelson was rated as a midshipman by his uncle as was usual for boys who were expected to become officers. Without the influential patronage Nelson had when he became a midshipman, it was extremely difficult, although not impossible, to rise from the lower decks to become an officer. The infamous Captain Bligh of 'Mutiny on the *Bounty*' fame was one such officer who made the transition. Nelson however was destined not to reach the Falkland Islands. Within a few weeks, by the time that the ship had been fitted out, Spain had withdrawn her force and *Raisonnable* was taken out of service. Luckily, Suckling was offered another command. Otherwise, Nelson would have been sent straight back home to Norfolk.

This second ship, however, still did not quite get Nelson to sea. It was the stationary 64 gun guardship, *Triumph* which protected the Medway and never actually went out to sea. Nelson learnt to pilot the ship's cutter along the Thames but, without seagoing experience, he had limited opportunity to learn his profession. To address this Suckling arranged for him to sail for a year with a merchantman which traded out of Florida, Bermuda and the Lesser Antilles. It is not known precisely where Nelson went or what the name of the ship was, although the Master had previously served with his uncle. Nelson wrote of his experience:

'I returned a practical seaman with a horror of the Royal Navy and with a saying then constant with seamen, "Aft the most honour, forward the better man!".'

He had been influenced by the merchant seamen's fears of discipline in the Royal Navy. This experience must have contributed to his own style of command in later life since he was to have a reputation for inspiring enormous loyalty from his men, for compassion and a distaste for flogging (although he did sometimes use it as a punishment). Of course he also overcame his prejudice against the Royal Navy!

From the Frozen North to the East Indies

At the end of his year with the merchantman, Nelson returned to duty on board the *Triumph*. He had remained on the ship's book which was a standard practice, or an accepted scam, in the Navy at that time. The reason for it was that a boy had to have six years of experience at sea before he could progress and take the examination to become a lieutenant. However he did not stop on the guardship for very long. In 1773, he was to get his first real taste of a naval expedition. Midshipman Nelson was accepted aboard the *Carcass* under Captain Skeffington Lutwidge. It was an expedition to the North Pole with the purpose of collecting astronomical information for the Royal Society. The wider aim of the voyage was to discover a northwest passage to the east for which George II had offered a substantial reward that was still waiting to be claimed.

At the beginning of June *Carcass* set sail together with the *Racehorse* which was captained by the leader of the venture, Constantine Phipps. The two ships had both been specially prepared for their destination with thickened hulls and buttressed bows so that they could cope with the pressure of ice. There were double rations of wine and spirits for the cold. Just in case the ships were lost they also carried bricks so that shelters could be built on the frozen land. Despite all the forethought, the expedition ran into trouble within a few weeks of reaching Spitzbergen. The ice to the north was so severe that the sea was blocked and the ships were trapped and in danger of being crushed. Strong winds began to blow the ice floes apart and the ships quickly took advantage of this to escape back south to the safety of Spitzbergen. Overall the expedition failed to fulfil any of its objectives but for Nelson it was not a total loss. He was captivated by the beauty of the region and the wildlife. He also caught the notice of his captain. He wanted to take a polar bear skin back for his father and set off with a fellow shipmate in the middle of the night. They duly found a bear but Nelson's musket misfired and he was ready to attack with the butt of the gun. At this moment he was separated from the bear when a chunk of ice broke away. This probably saved his life. He was reprimanded on return to the vessel, because he had ignored the Captain's call to return. Yet, overall, Nelson had a good report from the captain of his ship. Even this incident showed his fighting spirit, as well as his propensity to disobey orders. He was still only 15 years old.

When Nelson returned it was again his Uncle Maurice who managed the next stage of his career. Through Maurice's patronage Nelson was found a place on a twenty-one gun frigate, the *Seahorse*. This time he was to go east – for the first and the last time in his life. He said himself that he visited almost every part of the East Indies, from Bengal to Bussorah. Another first and last during this voyage was his experience of gambling at cards – he won £300. Since the pay of a midshipman at this time was around £60 per annum, this was a considerable sum but, when Nelson thought of what he could have lost, he resolved never to play again.

Like many of Nelson's early voyages this one was not to run smoothly. He became extremely ill with the malaria which was to recur throughout his life. It was arranged for him to return home, virtually dying, on the *Dolphin*. It was fortunate that the ship needed to stop at Simonstown in Africa for a month for repairs, as this meant that fresh food was available and the ship was able to replenish its supplies. The nutrients undoubtedly contributed to Nelson's eventual recovery, although he was at a low ebb:

'I felt impressed with a feeling that I should never rise in my profession. My mind was staggered with a view of the difficulties I had to surmount and the little interest I possessed. After a long and gloomy reverie, in which I almost wished myself overboard, a sudden glow of patriotism was kindled within me and presented my King and Country as my patron. Well then, I will be a hero, and, confiding in Providence, I will brave every danger.'

When he says 'little interest' he means that he did not have a wide circle of influential men who could advance his career.

Promotions and Patronage

When the ship got back to England things immediately looked brighter for Nelson's future. His uncle had been made Comptroller of the Navy, and, as such, was also the chairman of the Navy Board which was responsible for the management of the dockyards and the appointment of warrant officers. Next to the First Lord of the Admiralty it was one of the most influential positions in the navy. It was rather a surprise appointment since it usually went to a very senior officer, and it is not known how Suckling had so impressed the then First Lord, Lord Sandwich (the man after whom sandwiches were named because of his habit of having his meat between slices of bread when reluctant to leave the gambling table). However, for Nelson, it was a godsend. Since the navy operated on the system of patronage, he was now in a very strong position. The First Lord was unlikely to ignore any request from his comptroller. Indeed, as soon as Nelson was signed off the *Dolphin*, he was appointed acting lieutenant to the 64 gun *Worcester*. The mission this time was to convoy merchant ships back and between Gibraltar and the North Sea.

The captain of the *Worcester* put Nelson forward by introducing him to the port admiral and taking him to dinner with the Mayor of Portsmouth. Nelson also proved himself professionally, the captain expressing complete confidence in him when he was placed on watch. Nelson's rank of acting lieutenant could not be confirmed because it was necessary for him to pass an examination to be a full lieutenant and this was his next step when he returned to England.

The examination was taken in the presence of three captains and was administered by the navy board. His uncle was the chairman of the panel that Nelson was to face and the story goes that he did not disclose the identity of his nephew until he had passed the test. This seems a little unlikely as nepotism was neither unusual nor frowned upon. The source of the story is again the biography written a year after Nelson's death and presumably it was told to demonstrate that, despite his connections, the young man truly passed on merit. It was not a point that needed to be made. In his time at sea Nelson had received good reports from all his captains and had practised his seafaring skills under a wide range of circumstances. In theory, he should have failed the test because he was not yet 19 and, to pass, he should have been at least 20 years old. It was not a problem – ignoring the age restriction was another common example of the bending of the rules at the time. Nelson's connections did stand him in good stead in one respect. He was given a commission the very next day as a second lieutenant. Some officers could wait for years for a position, despite having passed the examination. Nelson was also lucky because it was a time of high employment in the navy. The British were fighting the American rebel colonies in the American War of Independence and, in 1778, war was declared on the French when they signed a pact in support of the Americans.

Nelson was assigned to the *Lowestoffe* which was bound for the Jamaica station, an important strategic base. His first duty was to command a press-gang to bring the ship up to a full complement. In theory, any seaman or waterman could be impressed by the gang, as well as anyone else who appeared of sufficient strength and forced to work at sea. In reality, those who had never been to sea were much less likely to be seized for no tight naval ship wanted a large number of unskilled and uninitiated crewmen. If an insufficient number of men were recruited in this way the crew was sometimes supplemented by criminals, sentenced to a term on board a ship rather than in prison. One evening, while in charge, Nelson collapsed with another attack of malaria and was returned to the ship. The ship's captain, Locker, made the decision to keep him with the ship in the hope that he would make a swift recovery. Locker liked to have portraits painted of his young officers and so, before they left, Nelson also sat for artist John Francis Rigaud, an Associate of the Royal Academy. When the ship departed for Jamaica the portrait was left unfinished. It was not to be completed for another three years.

Nelson got on extremely well with Locker, starting a friendship that would last until Locker's death. It was not long before he was over his illness and distinguishing himself on board. In rough seas the ship managed to overtake an American merchantman in an eight-hour chase, and it was the expected duty of the first lieutenant to board and secure the prize. In a story that Nelson was fond of repeating, the first lieutenant delayed and the captain shouted 'Have I no officer in this ship who can board the prize?' Nelson immediately took action and boarded and made a success of the operation. Later he wrote that 'this little incident has often occurred to my mind. I know it is in my disposition that difficulties and dangers do but increase my desire of attempting them'.

Locker demonstrated his trust in Nelson's ability by giving his young officer command of a captured schooner, which he re-named *Little Lucy* after his daughter. This gave Nelson a taste of independent command. He also caught the eye of Rear Admiral Sir Peter Parker who was sent out to command at Port Royal in Jamaica. Although Nelson was building up a good reputation on his own merits, Parker's interest in him may also have been aroused by his knowledge that his uncle was Comptroller of the Navy! In a classic move to bring on young officers, Parker took Nelson into his flagship *Bristol,* as third lieutenant, and he subsequently became the first lieutenant. He had not been with *Bristol* for very long when he was given command of the *Badger* brig and sent to protect the Mosquito shoreline and the Bay of Honduras from American privateers. Again he shone – this time preventing tragedy by saving the crew of another British ship, the *Glasgow*, which had caught fire. Fire was a huge risk on board wooden ships. Since there was nowhere to run on a ship and most sailors of the period were unable to swim, it was a terrifying prospect at sea.

It was fortunate that Nelson had forged such strong relationships with Locker and Parker. Just as he joined Parker's ship, he heard that his Uncle Maurice Suckling had died. Parker was now his main patron.

At the end of the mission Nelson was to learn that he had been 'made post'. In other words, he had been promoted to captain and was to command the frigate *Hinchinbrooke*. This was his first real step towards a major command. At twenty-one Nelson was very young for a post captain. Most officers gained such a position in their late twenties or early thirties.

The Nicaraguan Expedition

By now, in 1779, there was widespread war, with two more of Britain's traditional enemies entering the fray. The Spanish had declared war in the Americas alongside the French, in return for the promise of French assistance in regaining control of Gibraltar and Florida. The Dutch too had signed a treaty of amity with the American rebels.

The West Indies, where Nelson was posted with the *Hinchinbrooke*, was an extremely important British strategic base, and the French had already taken St Vincent and Grenada. It was expected that the French Vice-Admiral Comte d'Estaing would attack Jamaica with a significant force and Nelson was given command of Fort Charles, a battery at Port Royal which, in his own estimation, was the most important post on the whole island. The French outnumbered the British and, in a letter home, Nelson wrote that 'I think you must not be surprised to hear of my learning to speak French'. Presumably he was anticipating becoming a prisoner of war. However the danger passed without an attack. D'Estaing was sent to aid the Americans in Savannah. At Spain's declaration of war Nelson went to patrol the Central American coast until returning to Jamaica at the end of the year. Major-General Dalling, the governor of the island, had conceived a plan to divide the Spanish colonies in Central America in two by sending troops up the Nicaraguan River, the San Juan, then over to Lake Nicaragua and into Granada. The main obstruction, other than the dangers of disease and jungle navigation, was the Spanish fort, San Juan which lay approximately 65 miles up river.

Dalling had the support of the Secretary for the Colonies back in London, although Admiral Parker, aware of his limited naval resources and the inherent dangers of the trip, was very much against the plan. Nelson, however, was enthusiastic and Parker sanctioned his participation, especially since, by now, Nelson had a good knowledge of that particular coastline. He was appointed to escort troops to the mouth of the San Juan, which, although their departure had been delayed by difficulties in recruiting reinforcements, they reached safely. Camp was set up at the mouth of the river where Nelson was due to return to base. However there was considerable difficulty navigating the smaller craft, into which the supplies had been reloaded, up river. Because some of the canoes were top heavy, the medical supplies were left behind. This was extremely unfortunate since the camp was set on swampy ground rife with mosquitoes and there was the danger of malaria. Nelson took it upon himself to continue on the expedition to help with the navigation and kept 50 crew members from *Hinchinbrooke* with him. It would not be the last time that Nelson disobeyed orders in following his own initiative.

The delayed departure made matters worse since it meant that they were going up river near the end of the dry season. The water was so low that the men had to drag the boats over mud. They also had to contend with tropical rainstorms and alligators, and at least one man was lost to a snake bite. Almost as soon as they arrived Nelson was again crippled with stomach pains. He had symptoms of dysentery which was thought to be caused by drinking water from a clear pool which had a branch of the poisonous machineel tree floating in it. In addition, he was suffering from malaria. Admiral Parker unwittingly saved Nelson's life by sending orders up river, instructing him to return and take command of the 44 gun frigate *Janus*. Nelson was transported by canoe. Now that the water was flowing freely again, the return journey took just three days, in comparison to the three weeks that it had taken to get there. In Kingston, Cuba Wallis, a freed Jamaican slave, cared for him which also contributed to his ultimate survival – the individual attention and herbal preparations Wallis gave had better results than anything Nelson might have had in a local hospital. Nelson's recovery was once again slow and he was moved to Admiral Parker's house in the mountains where the climate was less harsh.

Back in San Juan the Fort surrendered shortly after Nelson's departure, but the toll in men was very high. As Dalling's ambitious Nicaraguan expedition came to an end the *Hinchinbrooke* had lost all but ten of its 200-strong crew to disease.

Once it was established that Nelson was unable to

take command of the *Janus* because of his illness he was sent back to England – the second time that he was sent home apparently close to death. The immediate future was to prove enormously frustrating for him. He would have to wait another thirteen years to be offered a ship of equivalent calibre.

'I return to England hope revives within me,' he wrote, 'I shall recover and my dream be fulfilled. Nelson will yet be an Admiral. It is the climate that has destroyed my health and crushed my spirit. Home and dear friends will restore me.'

Nelson joined his hypochondriac father who, not for the first time, was taking the waters at Bath. Despite his characteristic optimism and pride, the younger Nelson still had to be carried to his bed in the late autumn of that year. By the end of January 1781, he was eager to take another command even though he had still not recovered the use of his left arm. He wrote to Locker, 'My health thank God, is very nearly perfectly restored; and I have the perfect use of all my limbs except my left arm, which I can hardly tell what is the matter with it. From the shoulder to my fingers' ends are as if half dead but the surgeons and doctors give me hopes it will all go off. I most sincerely wish to be employed, and hope it will not be long.'

By May, having suffered a mild relapse, he still had no feeling in the arm and was also troubled by the loss of movement in his left leg. This did not stop him seeking re-employment and, from his position at the Customs Office, William Suckling (Maurice's brother) lobbied Charles Jenkinson, the Secretary of War, on his behalf. In turn, Jenkinson wrote to Sandwich and Nelson also had glowing reports from both Dalling and Parker. Sandwich promised a command as soon as one was available but perhaps it was better for Nelson, in his still delicate state, that one was not yet vacant. He used his time to visit his brothers in Burnham Thorpe and he also returned to Rigaud's studio for the completion of the portrait started three years earlier. Nelson wrote to Locker, who commissioned the portrait, 'It will not be in the least like I am now, but you may tell Mr Rigaud to add beauty, and it will be much mended'.

His face had to be made thinner and his uniform was changed to reflect his status as a captain. In addition Rigaud depicted the captured fort of San Juan in the background to reflect Nelson's latest success. The completed portrait hung in Locker's dining-room in Greenwich until he died and left it to Nelson's brother William. It now hangs at the National Maritime Museum in Greenwich. This painting was one of approximately 45 images of Nelson made in his lifetime and there were of course even more after his death. Apart from Queen Victoria and the Duke of Wellington, Nelson's portrait was painted more often than any other national figure in the nineteenth century.

In August 1781 Nelson was back at sea in the *Albemarle*, a 28 gun frigate. She was not as impressive as the *Janus* but he was satisfied with her. He was to spend the winter in the North Sea, and had to supplement his crew by chasing an East Indiaman in the Thames Estuary in order to seize more men. He was still not fully fit and, by 21 October, on arrival at the Nore, he was hardly able to get out of bed. In spite of this he was ordered to command two additional frigates in order to escort a merchant convoy consisting of 260 ships coming from the Baltic back to England. The cargo included essential supplies for the Navy. The convoy was safely taken into Great Yarmouth, but a couple of weeks later *Albemarle* was accidentally run into by a merchant vessel and Nelson had to stay in Portsmouth for four months while the ship underwent repairs. On completion the ship was sent to Quebec to escort another convoy. Nelson was hungry to take prizes – to capture enemy vessels. Sailors who captured a prize were entitled to a share of the profits which often amounted to more than a year's salary. A modest capture of a ship, worth, say, £10,000, would net the captain around £2,500, lieutenants £310 and an ordinary seaman £25. In the course of the voyage, Albemarle took an American schooner and a French frigate.

In September, when Nelson was staying in Quebec, he started an affair with a reputed local beauty, Mary Simpson, which appears to have been his first significant dalliance. He had to be persuaded by a friend to continue with his orders to escort troops to New York, rather than to stay and make a marriage proposal. Whether it was the romance or not, Nelson recovered his health and he felt better than ever. New York also threw him in the path of Admiral Hood, fresh from victories against the French and, like Admiral Rodney back in England, something of a national hero. Both of them had just been knighted and had achieved the kind of glory for which Nelson was eager. Sailing with Lord Hood was George III's third son, Prince William, and Nelson managed to impress them both, so much so that Hood requested that the *Albemarle* return with him to his West Indies station. Almost immediately, Nelson repaid their confidence by taking a French transport ship loaded with masts, a commodity which the Royal Navy badly needed. The American war was coming to a close and Nelson now made another bid for recognition by bringing together a squadron to attempt to recapture the tiny Turk's Island in the Bahamas, which had been taken by the French. However the island was well protected and peace was imminent. Nelson had to give up the plan. Essentially, the war had been good for his career, in terms of promotion and the good contacts that he had made. In 1783, after the signing of the Peace of Paris, Nelson returned to England and the *Albemarle* was signed off at Spithead with all the crew offering to follow Nelson to another ship. Although this was unlikely to happen, it demonstrated the excellent leadership skills the young Nelson had developed. He truly had the ability to inspire.

The West Indies and Marriage

A New Command

Now that England was at peace, having lost the American colonies but maintained her interest in the West Indies, the Navy was reducing the number of active ships and Nelson was unemployed on half pay. He took the opportunity to visit his family at Burnham Thorpe and then, with a fellow officer, he decided to go and live in France, ostensibly to learn the language. This may have been suggested to him as a career move since French publishing on naval matters was at the forefront at the time. However, the young man did not make the most of the opportunity, instead spending his time enjoying himself and womanising. He hoped to marry one of the women he met – Elizabeth Andrews, the daughter of a clergyman. Financially, however, Nelson was not in a good position to marry. After appealing to his uncle for an allowance, without success, he had to tell Miss Andrews that he was not ready for marriage and he returned to England.

Back in London, he began campaigning immediately to obtain another command – socialising with

Lord Howe, now First Lord of the Admiralty, and with Lord Hood. The strategy paid off and he was appointed to the *Boreas* frigate of 28 guns. He was fortunate in the appointment as peacetime commands were hard to come by, especially for a young officer without seniority. The Navy List was ordered by age and, once one was a captain, promotion was automatic as those at the top died and vacancies became available. 'Seniority' was the term used to express an officer's placing on the list. Although Nelson had made a good account of himself the appointment to *Boreas* still owed more to patronage than to merit alone.

The time that Nelson spent with *Boreas* was not to be his finest or happiest hour in command. He was posted again to the West Indies but the ship ran aground leaving England and departure was delayed by a day. Nelson was furious with the pilot. Then, before leaving British waters the ship was caught in a gale and in a quarrel with a Dutch East Indiaman, whose captain made a complaint against Nelson. However Nelson's conduct was backed by the Admiralty and finally *Boreas* was under way.

The young captain was unhappy with the number of passengers that he had to take on the ship. With over thirty on the quarterdeck, it was far too crowded. He had a goodly number of lieutenants, most of whom he had taken on to please friends and patrons. His brother William was also part of the ship's company, having decided to try his hand as a naval chaplain. The guests also included Lady Hughes and her daughter, the family of the Controller in Chief on the West Indies station. Nelson found Lady Hughes particularly irksome, referring to her as a great 'clack'. If her incessant chatter was not enough, the Captain spent over £200 in entertaining her and her daughter, at the end of which she gave him only a five shilling gift of a silver tea caddy spoon.

Disagreements and Dissensions

Nelson's dissatisfaction was not to end when the ship arrived in Jamaica. He was missing the society of his colleague Collingwood, who was in Grenada, and found no-one else to take his place. However, he truly enjoyed the company of Mrs Moutray, the wife of the dockyard commissioner in Antigua. Nelson wrote to Locker that, 'Was it not for Mrs Moutray who is very, very good to me, I should almost hang myself at this infernal hole'. His friendship with her would result in a correspondence that lasted the rest of his life. It also seems that he fell in love with her. When she left the island with her husband he fancied that all the trees around her former home were drooping in mourning. There is no suggestion that any liaison occurred – reputedly, she was a loving wife and she was an even greater intimate of Collingwood than she was of

Nelson – but there was considerable affection between them, which remained unaltered even when Nelson was in dispute with her husband. In fact, during his time on the station, Nelson managed to have a dispute with almost everyone other than Mrs. Moutray.

Nelson was irritated with Moutray for flying a commodore's pennant, as the rank is only a temporary one in the Navy. In addition to this, Moutray was now in a civilian position in the dockyard. Nelson therefore refused to follow any orders that Moutray might issue. Technically, Nelson was in the right but he rather overstated his case. He clashed with Hughes over the issue of illegal American traders to which Hughes and other commanders tended to turn a blind eye. Nelson was not at all diplomatic in his complaints and, in fact, ended up by sounding rather pompous, 'How the King's attorney-general conceives he has a right to give an illegal opinion, which I assert the above is, he must answer for. I know the navigation law.'

To an extent, Nelson must have been aware of the precarious position that he was putting himself in with the Admiralty, although he wrote to them, with a degree of self-righteousness, that 'I stand for myself; no great connections to support me if inclined to fall; therefore my good name as a man, an officer and an Englishman, I must be very careful of. My greatest pride is to dislodge my duty faithfully, my greatest ambition to receive approbation for my conduct'.

Nelson's insistence on battling with American traders led to his confinement on his ship for some weeks in order to avoid arrest. Several merchants and ship-owners had taken out writs against him but, on board, he was immune from them. This meant that he could only safely go out on Sundays, on one of which he met his future wife Frances Nisbet on the island of Nevis.

Fanny Nisbet

Fanny Nisbet was the daughter of William Woodward, the senior judge in Nevis. She was the widow of Dr Josiah Nesbit who had been her father's doctor and who had died after a short illness when they moved back to England and to Salisbury. Fanny returned to Nevis, together with her three-year-old son, Josiah, and acted as the housekeeper to her maternal uncle, Mr Herbert, the president of the island's council. It was Josiah who really helped to break the ice between Nelson and the family. Nelson had been a regular vis-itor to the house but he had been rather sombre and Mr Herbert was astonished one Sunday. As he re-ported in a letter, 'Great God if I did not find that great little man of whom everyone is so afraid, playing in the next room, under the dining table with Mrs Nisbet's child.'

It was the spring of 1785 and, by August, Nelson was writing to Fanny as if she had already accepted a pro-

posal, talking of sharing his money and living in a cottage together. It seems that Nelson had already made up
his mind and he was keen to obtain the blessing of Mr
Herbert. He did not need his permission but, while
Nelson had no money, Mr Herbert was a rich man and
Fanny a potential heiress. In all, over the following year
and a half, Nelson made seven applications to Herbert
about his possible marriage. Herbert seems not to have
been against the marriage in principle and remained be-
nign and courteous but he advocated delay. Perhaps he
was testing Nelson's commitment to his niece but the
most likely explanation is that he was unwilling to lose
his housekeeper. Nelson persisted and, in addition, ap-
pealed once more to his uncle Suckling for an allowance which was granted.

History has not been very kind to Fanny Nisbet,
seeing her as cold, and certainly she pales in comparison with Nelson's mistress, the flamboyant Lady
Hamilton. However, there seems to have been genuine affection on both sides. Nelson's letters to her are
gossipy and look forward to a future together. It is
true that they do not have the explicitness and near
abandon of some of his letters to Emma Hamilton,
and they are sometimes hardly different in style to
those that he wrote to close friends. She was certainly
less extrovert than Emma, but that could be said of
many. Fanny's reputation for coldness is derived
largely from a biography of Nelson, written by James

Harrison in 1806 just after his death. Harrison had been befriended by Emma Hamilton, then trying to forward her own cause in trying to obtain a pension from the government. Harrison had access to Emma's memories and some of her letters, and Emma, perhaps not surprisingly, did not present Fanny in a good light. In addition to this, most of the correspondence between Nelson and Fanny was lost until 1898, and not published until 1958. The surviving letters are also rather one-sided since Nelson habitually burnt letters that he received. Consequently it has been difficult to put together a representative picture of Fanny. She certainly seems to have been liked by her contemporaries and was adored by Nelson's father. One of the reasons that Nelson was initially so attracted to her was that she reminded him of Mrs Moutray. Because of this and the miserable time he was having in the West Indies, he may have been disposed to like her more than he might otherwise have done. Even so, it was two years from the time they met until they finally married and there is no evidence of any change in his feelings during that period.

While Nelson was creating controversy in the West Indies he also met up with Prince William again and this was not a friendship which improved his standing with the Admiralty. Now captaining his own ship, the Prince was a capricious and strict captain and was not in command of a happy crew. The Prince's temporary influence on Nelson's style of command was a negative one. They spent their time partying and Nelson was exhausted by the Prince's energy. The two men became sufficiently close for William to want to attend Nelson's wedding to Fanny – indeed, he wanted to give the bride away. As usual, Nelson was impressed by the Prince's status and, in these circumstances, his judgement was likely to be impaired. He was unaware that the King and the government had conspired together to keep the Prince occupied and out of trouble by finding him employment in the Navy. Nelson thought that the Prince's virtues outweighed his faults, but William was a very young captain in his first command and already in dispute with his efficient first lieutenant, Schomberg. This came to a head when the lieutenant sent a boat ashore without the express permission of the Captain. The Prince was heavy-handed, sending a written warning for neglect of duty, for what was really a very minor incident. It was not the first time the two men had clashed and Schomberg asked for a court martial so that he might clear his name. As the senior captain, it was Nelson who put him under arrest and the Prince intended trying Schomberg for mutiny after the court martial. The whole matter was diplomatically resolved by Commodore Alan Gardner, who managed to get Schomberg to withdraw his request for a court martial and moved him to another ship.

Marriage and Unemployment

Nelson married Fanny in Montpelier on 11 March 1787 – the date was set by Prince William – before the Nelsons returned to England in June 1787. They travelled separately, Nelson in the *Boreas* and Fanny with her uncle on a West Indiaman. They had to wait to set up home together because the *Boreas* was not paid off until later in the year, and Nelson was having a difficult time with the aftermath of events in the Caribbean. The ship was not a happy one and this time no-one volunteered to follow him to his next command. He was in trouble with the Admiralty for having allowed the Prince to sail to Halifax by way of Jamaica, and for having authorized him to refuse to submit a muster book to the clerk at the Antigua dockyard. Nelson must only have authorised this because of his obsequious regard for the Prince. It is hard to imagine, bearing in mind his usual judgement and attention to detail, that he would have tolerated such a breach from anyone else. This was not the end of the Admiralty's questions. Nelson had also made some promotions of men which the Admiralty would not confirm. Nelson was furious about this and worried how it would affect his reputation with officers. He had also pardoned a man for desertion (his boatswain who was reputedly insane) but, rather than bring him back to Britain, had appointed him as a sail maker's assistant at the Antigua dockyard, an appointment he had no authority to make. In the mean time, Nelson was continuing to stir up trouble by writing numerous letters, making allegations of fraud in the West Indies' dockyards. England was again largely at peace with her rivals and there were few commands to be had. Nelson was by no means improving his chances of getting one of them.

He must have been relieved when the *Boreas* was finally signed off in November 1787. Without a new ship he was put on half pay and reunited with Fanny. With no house of their own, they moved into the parsonage at Burnham Thorpe with Nelson's father, with whom Fanny immediately established a close rapport. Partly as a result of this good relationship, they stayed in Norfolk although it had been their intention to move to France. Fanny spoke French reasonably well and the idea was for Nelson to make another attempt to learn it. However, they would stay at Burnham Thorpe for another three years, Nelson helping out on the land, and it would be five years before he got another command. This was a source of enormous frustration to him, but it was not an unusual situation. Another great admiral, Lord St Vincent, once had to wait for seven years. Nelson's failure to get another command was not entirely due to his recent behaviour. In times of peace there were always more officers than ships. In reality, he had been very fortunate to have had five commands to his credit already.

In 1790 a fleet was put together, as a possible war with Spain threatened, and Nelson was disappointed to be overlooked. The influence of the Prince seemed to count for very little. Nelson called on Lord Hood at the Admiralty and was truly distraught when he was told that the King did not look favourably upon him. Nelson had also failed, despite his continued friendship with William, to gain a place in the Prince's household for Fanny.

War Against the French

In 1792, relations with France again worsened and this provided Nelson with another opportunity. Finally, he got the call to the Admiralty for which he had been so desperate. He was back in favour and, in January 1793, he got a commission to the *Agamemnon* of 64 guns in Lord Hood's Mediterranean fleet, a ship the men nicknamed 'eggs and bacon'. (Nelson was offered a ship of 74 guns if he was prepared to wait, but characteristically he was eager to get straight into action.) His letters to Fanny at the time were full of his excitement. She was, of course, lonely – in addition to going himself, Nelson had taken her son Josiah with him as a midshipman, as well as a young Suckling cousin. Just before Nelson was ready to depart Mr Herbert died. Fanny did not inherit his fortune since he had been reconciled with his daughter but he did leave the Nelsons some money. The fact that Fanny's inheritance was smaller than originally expected probably influenced the decision to take Josiah to sea, since entering him into another profession would have been difficult without more money. Certainly Josiah's naval career does not seem to have been planned before, since Nelson could, if he had wished, have already put the lad's name down in the books of the *Boreas* when he was seven.

With both of those closest to her at the mercy of the sea, Fanny was constantly worried about her family. So she was not really able to share in Nelson's obvious enthusiasm. Her husband was also frustrated with her for not sending all of his belongings to the ship and he scolded her for packing some of the things that did arrive very poorly. Although these facts have been used to show the beginnings of cracks in their relationship, they seem fairly minor things after six years of marriage. However, her inability to share Nelson's eagerness for action and glory, though understandable, was a bad sign for the future since it was such a motivating force for him and he enjoyed, and needed, constant approval. In terms of his career the next four years would bring him the recognition and glory he craved and this, in turn, would lead to a much greater confidence in his own judgement as a commander.

Nelson's orders were to cruise in the Channel be-

fore joining Hood in Toulon. He could not see the reason for cruising – he realised later that it was because
it would take sometime for the fleet to group together
and the Western Approaches needed to be protected –
but he learnt something from the experience. When
he was later a commander in chief he would take his
junior captains into his confidence so that, knowing
the overall plan, they would be better equipped to
make informed decisions. Nelson visited Hood on
board his flagship *Victory* and was delighted to find that
the meeting was cordial. In fact, he was chosen to lead
one of the fleet's three divisions. He was also offered a
74 gun ship but turned it down, preferring to stay
with the officers in the *Agamemnon*. It was a happy ship
and Nelson had found his feet again as a successful and
popular captain.

In August, Nelson was dispatched to Naples and
made an appeal to King Ferdinand IV to supply troops
to help the allied forces (British, Spanish, Sardinian
and French loyalist) to hold the French naval base
which was in danger of being overtaken by the French
republican army. It was in Naples that he would first
meet Emma Hamilton when he had to deliver his
despatches to Sir William Hamilton, her husband and
the British envoy. Nelson was impressed by both husband and wife. Persuaded by Nelson, Sir William and
John Acton, an expatriate who had become principal
minister in the Naples court, the King made a prom-

ise to supply 4,000 troops for Toulon, even before Hood's official order had arrived. Nelson, possessed of considerable charm that he could use to his advantage, acquired a taste for such negotiation.

He returned briefly to Toulon, which was under fire, before Hood sent him to Cagliari via Corsica to join Commodore Linzee. He was quickly into action, pursuing three French frigates on the Sardinian coast. Nelson went after the closest despite the fact that *Agamemnon*, which had left some of its crew ashore in Toulon, was short-handed. He engaged the French *Melpomene* for around four hours, seriously damaging her. Unfortunately a wind change prevented him from finishing the job though, interestingly, he consulted his officers before making the final decision to end the chase. He was maturing as a leader. It was a time of non-stop action and Nelson thrived on it. His orders first took him to Tunis to help persuade the Dey to give a French fleet of Levant merchantmen into British hands. Next he was sent to Italy to command a small squadron protecting British trade coming into the Gulf of Genoa and to take enemy ships.

The allies were unable to hold Toulon and the British were forced to find another base. The plan was to secure Corsica. It was the obvious choice and the patriot leader Paoli, who had already organised resistance to the French, was in favour of British allegiance. This is where Nelson next went, anchoring off

Maginaggio, a small village where the French revolutionary flag was flying. He sent word that he had come to deliver the residents from the republicans. He struck down the flag himself and went on to the larger towns of Bastia and Calvi. By this time there were major disagreements between the army and the navy. The navy's plan was to storm the towns whereas the army wanted to use blockade. Hood claimed he was the supreme commander but the army officers denied this. Nelson, as usual, was even more eager than Hood, and showed his usual enthusiasm for land campaigns. He was to be in charge of all naval forces on land and he was keen to prove himself again and to go as far as was necessary, writing to Fanny that a brave man only died once but a coward all his life long. After a five-week siege, Bastia was starved out and surrendered. Almost immediately the forces moved on to Calvi, which they intended to bombard, and Nelson was put in charge of placing the guns. This was a dangerous process as the men were in the range of the enemy guns on the city walls. It was also exhausting as the ground was rough, rocky and uphill. There were many casualties, including Nelson himself who was wounded on 12 July. It was not a direct hit but shot landing on the ground threw up stone and sand which cut and bruised his face and also permanently damaged his right eye. At first, he could only distinguish dark and light but it grew worse. The eye stayed in almost total darkness and caused much pain during an-other slow recovery. His attitude is shown in a letter home. 'But never mind,' he wrote, 'I can see very well with the other.' What caused him far more consterna-tion was that, although he had been instrumental in bringing Corsica under British control, the London papers barely mentioned his exploits. He often wrote to Fanny at this time complaining of the lack of recog-nition that he received. He felt even worse when Hood, with whom he had built up a relationship of mutual respect and esteem, was replaced by Admiral Hotham.

The winter of 1794 saw the *Agamemnon* in Leghorn, a convenient shelter while the fleet blockaded Toulon. Here Nelson met Adelaide Correglia, an opera singer, with whom he had an affair, although he continued to write with affection to Fanny. The affair was not very discreet and one of Nelson's fellow officers, Captain Freemantle, commented that 'he makes himself ridiculous with this woman'. He would encounter similar criticism in his relationship with Emma Hamilton. However, in terms of his career, it was now that he really began to establish his reputation for bravery and willingness to die for his cause. In March 1795 the French fleet left port and the British gave chase.

The chase only gave rise to minor action as the British were unable to engage the French fully in battle. Nelson managed to disable the *Ca Ira*, an 80 gun ship, when it collided with another vessel, firing broadsides through her stern. The French fleet turned back in order to support the *Ca Ira* and Hotham ordered Nelson to retreat. The following day the ship struck her colours along with the *Censeur* which had been towing her when both of them had lost their masts. There was a general chase but the wind meant that the French kept their distance. In Nelson's opinion Hotham did not give him full credit for taking the *Ca Ira*, mentioning him only once in his official report, and he complained bitterly to Fanny about the incident, as well as Hotham's caution in attack.

'I wish to be an Admiral and in command of the English fleet. I should very soon either do much or be ruined. My disposition cannot bear tame and slow measures. Sure I am, had I commanded out fleet on the 14th, that either the whole French fleet would have graced my triumph, or I should have been in a confounded scrape. I went on board Hotham so soon as our firing grew slack in the van, and the *Ca Ira* and *Censeur* struck, to propose to him leaving our two crippled ships, the two prizes, and four frigates, to themselves and to pursue the enemy, but he is much cooler than myself and said "We must be contented. We have done very well," but had we taken 10 sail and allowed the 11th to have escaped if possible to have been got at, I could never call it well done. Goodhall backed me. I got him to write to the Admiral, but it would not do. We should have had such a day as I believe the annals of England never produced but it can't be helped.'

Nelson was pleased when, in November 1795, Hotham was replaced by Sir John Jervis who was more appreciative of Nelson's propensity for action. He also felt that Jervis treated him more like an associate than a subordinate. Jervis sent Nelson to patrol the coast of Genoa and seize vessels of any nationality destined for France. It was a role that required considerable diplomacy since Genoa was neutral, but Nelson performed extremely well and Jervis gave him a larger ship, the 74 gun *Captain*, commended him to the Admiralty and appointed him commodore. This temporary rank gave him authority over specific ships. He was unwilling to apply for leave (as Fanny desperately wanted him to do) for fear that he would afterwards be posted to a different station and lose the advantageous position he was in with Jervis. Again he was anxious to publicise his actions and his confidence was at an all time high. In particular, he wanted his achievements written up in the *London Gazette*, and he wrote to Fanny:

'Had all my actions been gazetted not one fortnight would have passed. Let those enjoy their brag and one day or other I will have a large Gazette to myself. I feel that one day or other such an opportunity will be given me... Wherever there is anything to be done, there Providence is sure to direct my steps, and ever credit must be given me in spite of envy...'

These beliefs were the source of his energy and motivation, and even his sickly constitution seemed improved by his self-belief:

'God knows I shall come to not a sixpence richer than when I set out, but I verily believe with a much better constitution. If I ever feel unwell, it is when I have no active employment that is but seldom.'

Conquests in Love and War

Cape St Vincent

Overall, the war was going badly for the British. Spain was on the verge of changing sides, Napoleon was achieving success in Italy and Austria, and the previously safe port of Leghorn had been taken. At the end of September 1796 Nelson had to supervise the evacuation of Bastia and Elba, where he had only recently escorted troops. The government decided that they should withdraw homeward from the Mediterranean, believing that the combined strength of the French and Spanish fleets was too much. Nelson was furious at the decision:

'At home they know not what this fleet is capable of performing. Much as I rejoice to see England, I lament our present orders in sackcloth and ashes, so dishonourable to the dignity of England, whose fleets are equal to meeting the World in arms. To say I am grieved and distressed but ill describes my feelings.'

However the decision to return to England had unexpected consequences. Nelson sailed past Gibraltar into the Atlantic and sighted the Spanish fleet sailing westerly. He had to make a difficult decision – whether to find the rest of the British fleet to warn Jervis of the Spanish presence, or head for the West Indies to warn them there, should that be the destination of the Spanish. He decided upon Jervis and found him on 13 February 1797 sailing by St Vincent, Portugal. Through the mist they saw 27 Spanish ships. Jervis had only 16 under his command. The Spanish were sailing in two divisions and the British passed between the two. Jervis ordered his ships to turn about and engage the two groups separately. Nelson saw that, unless the British ships closed on the Spanish more quickly, the two enemy divisions would come together and combine their strength. He decided to act on his own initiative. He took the *Captain* out of the line and thrust it into the gap between the two halves of the Spanish fleet. This exposed him to seven Spanish ships including the *Santisima Trinidad* which was then the largest warship in the world.

Excellent commanded by Collingwood, *Culloden* under Troubridge and the *Blenheim* all went in support of Nelson and quickly they were all damaged. The *Captain* was disabled when her wheel and the rigging were smashed and Nelson ran her alongside the *San Nicolas*, the nearest Spanish vessel, and called for a boarding party which he joined himself, jumping through the stern windows of the ship with his sword drawn. The Spanish ensign was brought down and, although the *San Nicolas* was still firing at the British, several Spanish officers handed their swords to Nelson. At that moment the crew from the adjacent *San Josef* began firing at the boarding crew with muskets, killing seven of them. The *San Josef*'s rigging had become locked with that of the *San Nicolas* and so Nelson called for reinforcements to the boarding party and used the first ship as a bridge to board the second, even though the *San Josef* was now on fire.

'I directed my brave fellows to board this first-rate and it was done in a moment…It was not long before I was on the quarterdeck where the Spanish captain, with a bended knee, presented me with a sword and told me the Admiral was dying of his wounds below. I gave him my hand and desired him to call to his officers and ship's company that the ship had surrendered, which he did.'

The use of the first ship as a stepping stone to the second became known throughout the fleet as 'Nelson's Patent Bridge for Boarding First-Rates'. After returning to his ship and presenting his second-in-command with a sword in gratitude, he proceeded to see Jervis on board the *Victory*. Fresh from the battle he was still dishevelled, his uniform torn, his hat missing and his face smothered in gun powder. Jervis, by contrast, had probably changed into fresh clothes. Earlier in the day, a marine had had his head shot off beside him and the admiral had been so covered in

blood and brains that one of his officers had raced to
him, believing him injured. According to Nelson,
Jervis met him on the quarterdeck, 'and having em-
braced me, said he could not sufficiently thank me and
used every kind expression which could not fail to
make me happy'.

It was his biggest success so far and, characteristically, Nelson could not wait to publicise his part in it.
He wrote his own account of the action, signed by two
of his officers and sent it to Locker to be published in
the papers. The account caused a little controversy as
Vice Admiral William Parker contested Nelson's report of the part that his ship, the *Prince George*, had
played in the action and claimed that his own role in
damaging the *San Josef* had been underestimated. He
believed that the ship had already struck her colours
to him before Nelson took credit. Nelson wrote to
Parker to say that he was unaware of the *Prince George*
after she was called to stop firing when the *San Nicolas*
had surrendered, and so he could not enter a debate
about it. Nelson was not someone who liked to share
his glory with anyone else, but he could well have
been oblivious to the action of the *Prince George* since
he had been so deep in the battle himself and did not
have an overview of it. In naval warfare at the time,
the level of smoke and debris often made it difficult to
see even the other side of your own ship, and the battle had been a messy one.

Fame and Misfortune

Back in England there was the kind of recognition for which Nelson yearned. All of the captains were given a gold medal, Jervis was made Earl St Vincent with a £3000 annuity and Captain Caulder was knighted. Nelson, for his part, was made a Knight of the Bath. There was more good news for him too. Shortly before the news of the battle had been received, he had been promoted to Rear Admiral of the Blue. This was simply a coincidence as the appointment came through seniority on the Naval list, and was automatic. The title 'of the blue' was a relic from the seventeenth century when the Navy had been divided into three divisions, each with their own ensign — red, white and blue, with the red being the most senior.

Back in Bath, Nelson was being feted with songs about his achievements from ballad singers, as well as at the theatre, and his proud father was stopped in the street by people who wanted to offer their congratulations. He sent Fanny a copy of a ballad written by a sailor about his action:

> The brave hero, Old England's boast
> Grappled two ships along,
> Forced them to strike on their own coast
> And lasting laurels won.

Long will this fact in history shine;
'Give me' the fair sex say,
'A Nelson for my Valentine
On this auspicious day.'

He was given the freedom of the cities of Bath,
Bristol, Norwich and London. He was delighted and
revelled in his fame, citing many examples of it to
Fanny, although the kind side of his nature was also re-
vealed when he asked Fanny to arrange the purchase
of fifty good quality large blankets with a monogram
'N' on them to distribute amongst the poor in his
father's parish at Burnham Thorpe. Fanny, however,
was still constantly anxious for him and wrote that 'I
sincerely hope, my dear husband that all these wonder-
ful and desperate actions, such as boarding ships, you
will leave to others. With the protection of a Supreme
Being, you have acquired a character, or name, which
all hands agree cannot be greater, therefore rest satisfied.' It was simply not in his nature to rest satisfied. It
was indeed not usual for a commodore to board a ship
himself (it was generally left to the captains) but
Nelson could never resist involvement and this is one
of the reasons he was so popular with the men.

He was not able to offer Fanny any assurance that
he would keep himself out of danger, writing about
later events in 1797:

'In April I hoisted my flag as rear-admiral of the

blue, and was sent to bring down the garrison of Porto Ferrajo; which service I performed, I shifted my flag from the *Captain* to the *Theseus* on 27th May, and was employed in the command of the inner squadron in the blockade of Cadiz. It was during this period that perhaps my personal courage was more conspicuous than at any other part of my life. In an attack of the Spanish gunboats, I was boarded in my barge with its common crew of ten men…The Spanish barge rowed twenty-six oars, besides officers, thirty in the whole; this was a service hand to hand with swords.'

Nelson's life was saved twice by the bravery of his coxswain John Sykes. One of the crew reported how Sykes had put forward his own hand when he saw a blow about to fall that would have cut off Nelson's head, and was badly injured himself.

Jervis, now Earl St Vincent, praised the attack. It was important for him to keep up both morale and authority, since this was the time of the mutinies over pay and conditions for seamen that occurred first at Spithead and, more violently, at the Nore. It was a dangerous time too. The French had planned an invasion of Ireland but had to withdraw and it was widely believed that England would be next to be invaded. The discontent had spread to the fleet in Cadiz as men came out from England. Rumours of a planned mutiny on board the *St George* were swiftly dealt with by St Vincent who court-martialled the leaders and sentenced them to death. He refused to give them the five days they requested to prepare, fearing the influence they might have on others. They were executed the following day, which happened to be a Sunday when such sentences would usually not take place. Some objected to the day but Nelson was in full support of the Admiral saying that, 'Had it been Christmas Day instead of Sunday, I would have executed them'.

Nelson proposed an attack on the town of Santa Cruz in Tenerife as it was the last port used by the Spanish ships to stop for water on their return from the Caribbean, often with extremely valuable cargoes of silver from the mines in Spanish parts of the Americas on board. He hoped to be able to seize a galleon full of treasure. St Vincent gave his assent to the plan. Surprise would be essential as the town was known to be well-defended. Nelson had three ships of the line and four frigates and the plan was for Captain Troubridge to land 1,000 men but, on the morning of 21 July, there was a forceful inshore current that carried the landing craft past their target and warning guns were fired from the town. Troubridge had to recall the men and the attack was aborted, with all element of surprise lost. Nelson was determined to try again, this time on 24 July, taking command himself. He must have been motivated by pride since it was folly to think that it could succeed and even Nelson doubted that he would return. The landing craft headed straight in to the harbour and were immediately under heavy fire with the loss of many men. Nelson tried to land and was shot by a musket ball in his right elbow. Josiah Nisbet took care of him, by getting him back in the boat, putting on a tourniquet and ordering the boat back to the ship. Nelson had sufficient presence of mind to stop the boat to order the rescue of some men from a sinking cutter before proceeding to the *Theseus*. Once on board his right arm was immediately amputated above the elbow. The surgeon wrote in his log: 'Admiral Nelson. Compound fracture of the right arm by a musket ball passing through a little above the elbow, an artery divided: the arm was immediately amputated and opium was afterwards given.' The pain had been excruciating, but Nelson thought it came not so much from the saw but from the cutting with a cold knife. Henceforward, he ordered surgeons to heat their knives before operating. There was a suggestion that the arm should be embalmed and sent to England to be buried but Nelson said, 'Throw it into the hammock with the brave fellow that was killed beside me'.

Only 700 men had managed to land and the Spanish had reinforced the garrison with up to 8,000. The Spanish, of course, did not surrender but they did allow the British to return to their ships and the Spanish commander even allowed them provisions from Tenerife. Nelson was very grateful – he had lost

153 men – and sent a cask of beer and offered to take the Spanish despatches to Cadiz. Then he wrote his first letter with his left hand to St Vincent, praising his men, regretting the failure of the attack and worrying that he would now become a burden without his right arm. He also wrote to his wife:

'My dearest Fanny, I am so confident of your affection that I feel the pleasure you will receive will be equal whether my letter is wrote by my right hand or left. It was the chance of war and I have much reason to be grateful, and I know it will add much to your pleasure in finding that Josiah under God's providence was principally instrumental in saving my life. As to my health it was never better and now I hope soon to return to you, and my country I trust will not allow me any longer to linger in want of that pecuniary assistance which I have been fighting the whole war to preserve her. But I shall not be surprised to be neglected and forgot as I shall no longer be considered as useful. However I shall feel rich if I continue to enjoy your affection…'

His spirits lifted when he got a response from St Vincent saying, 'Mortals cannot command success. You and your companions have certainly deserved by the greatest degree of heroism and perseverance that was ever exhibited.' As to money, Nelson's hopes were fulfilled. With the award of a disability pension of £1000 per annum, as well as his salary and prize money, he was now able to buy a house. He bought one called Roundwood near Ipswich without having seen it. A plain house with grounds of 50 acres, it does not survive today, having been demolished in 1960.

After four and a half years he was finally reunited with Fanny who nursed him since the arm was not healing properly. The silk ligatures on the arteries had not come away and the wound had become infected and painful. Despite this he was very happy in his domestic situation. In addition he was popular among the crowds in London, where he went to be invested by the King with the Order of the Bath. Lemuel Abbot was commissioned to paint another portrait – this time with his right sleeve pinned across his chest. This was not the only change in his appearance. His cheeks had sunk because of lost teeth and he was very conscious of this, keeping his mouth closed when smiling. His brittle hair had turned virtually white and his injured eye was now fixed and misty. (Contrary to popular myth, Nelson never wore an eye patch to cover the injury, as the eye looked relatively normal.) Nelson was pleased with the portrait and, until 1992, it was considered by many as the closest likeness of him. But, in that year, a sketch in oils by John Hoppner was found beneath another layer of paint. It was a preliminary sketch for a portrait in the Royal Collection. The sketch is now held by the Royal Naval Museum in Portsmouth.

Soon after his recovery in December he was delighted to be commissioned once again to join St Vincent's fleet and sent out with a squadron in the Mediterranean to discover the plans of an expeditionary force preparing at Toulon, with General Bonaparte and 15 first rate vessels under Admiral Brueys. Nelson's mission caused some jealousy among his fellow officers – he was, after all, the most junior of St Vincent's flag captains. However, Nelson knew the area extremely well and St Vincent was in no doubt of his tenacity and determination to succeed. Near Toulon the British fleet missed the sailing of the French fleet because of a severe storm. The storm also seriously damaged Nelson's *Vanguard* – the topsail yard came down, killing two of the crew, and both the main topmast and the mizzen topmast were lost to the sea. By the time that *Vanguard* had been repaired the French had disappeared and Nelson had no clue as to their destination. On 5 June, he heard from a merchant ship that the French had been seen sailing southeasterly from the north of Corsica. This narrowed down Nelson's quest but not by much – they could have been heading for Sicily, Naples, Malta, Corfu or Egypt. Egypt was potentially a route into India for the French troops.

Nelson wrote to Sir William Hamilton at Naples in the hope that he could provide information, and also to Lady Hamilton. Considering that it had been five years since they met, he received a surprisingly affectionate note from her. Nelson received no further orders for three months and he was unaware that Bonaparte had taken Malta from the Knights of the Order of St John of Jerusalem and looted their treasure. Neither did he know that the French had picked up reinforcements in Elba and Genoa and now had troops numbering 50,000. It is likely that Nelson's ships passed the French on the night of 22 June, south of Sicily, but unfortunately the frigates that would have scouted for them had been lost in the storm that had so damaged his own ship. He wrote that, 'Was I to die this moment, *want of frigates* would be found on my heart'. Back at home the newspapers were losing confidence in Nelson's ability to succeed, and those who were jealous of the appointment were claiming that St Vincent should have gone after the French himself.

The Battle of the Nile

Nelson, using both his instinct and the information that he had been able to collect, concluded that the most likely destination was Egypt and, searching along the Italian coastline, found nothing. He backtracked towards Sicily where, in the Gulf of Messina, he discovered that the French had indeed been heading for Egypt. Finally, on 1 August, he located them, seeing French transports off Alexandria and the French fleet in Aboukir Bay. The excitement was palpable. Characteristically, now that they were in sight, he lost no time in preparing for battle, deciding to attack the French where they lay. At first glance the French position looked a strong one – Brueys had 13 warships in a line astern across the semi-circular bay, north to south, which were also protected by batteries on Aboukir Island. The other advantage to the bay was that, on the land side, it was very shallow so an attacking division would run the risk of being grounded. Nelson had 12 ships.

Nelson, in consultation with his captains, decided to attack the French van and centre, which, since none of them was familiar with the area, meant that they would have to risk the shoals and take soundings on their way. *Culloden* under Troubridge did indeed run aground and was unable to participate in the forthcoming battle. However, Nelson did have some considerable advantages which were key in the outcome of the battle. Firstly his precipitate action meant that Brueys was taken totally by surprise. The French admiral was also undermanned since many of his crew were on land digging wells and others were stationed to protect them from Bedouin attacks. When he realised that Nelson intended to attack that day he made a signal for his fleet to engage the British at anchor.

The French ships were also only at single anchor so

the British soon realised that, where the ships were able to swing, there was sufficient water for them to enter. *Goliath*, captained by Foley, went in first, followed by four others, and these ships manoeuvred round the head of the French line to position themselves between the French and the shore. Nelson and the five remaining ships positioned themselves on the outside of the French line towards the sea. There is some disagreement about how this decision, which was to prove crucial, was made and whether it was Nelson's or Foley's idea. Whatever the truth, Nelson had created a real team spirit among his captains and they worked together remarkably well to make the very most of this tactic.

The battle began as the sun set, the first cannon being fired at half past six. The French had not even had time to run out their guns on the land side. The British worked systematically through the night, first concentrating fire on the major French vessels, picking each one off before moving along the line to blast them all into submission. Only two French ships managed to escape by cutting their cables and sailing out to sea. By half past eight both Brueys and Nelson were injured. Brueys's wound was to prove fatal – a shot in the stomach nearly severed him in two and he lay dying on the quarterdeck. Nelson, hit by iron shrapnel, also believed that his injury was mortal. A flap of skin fell over his eye and, feeling the amount of blood that was flowing, he said to Berry who had caught him, 'I am killed; remember me to my wife'. He was taken below for the rest of the battle. Later Nelson remarked that, had he not been injured, the two French ships that escaped would never have got away. The whole British and French fleets were stunned into silence when, at around nine or ten, Admiral Brueys' flagship, the great *L'Orient* of 120 guns, exploded as fire reached her magazine. Only 70 of her 1000 crew survived. Nelson was able to go back out on deck when she caught fire, and felt sufficiently recovered to start writing his reports. By midnight it was all pretty much over and the British crews slept by their guns in exhaustion. In the morning the bay was awash with dead and mutilated bodies. The French had lost 3000 men with another 3000 taken prisoner; the British had lost about 1000.

It was a most resounding victory and one which changed the course of the Revolutionary War. The French Mediterranean fleet was effectively destroyed and Britain regained its supremacy in the Mediterranean. Not only that but the French army had also been marooned in Egypt.

The *Vanguard* was again in desperate need of repair and so Nelson set off for Naples, leaving some of his ships behind. He needed some attention himself – his recurring malaria had resurfaced and the recent wound was causing him excruciating migraines. He must nevertheless have been buoyed up as news of the great victory swept across Europe – the congratulations far exceeded the honours he had received after Cape St Vincent. He received many gifts including the famous chelengk (a jewelled plume) from the Sultan of Ottoman Turkey. At home he was made a baron. He had been hoping for the higher rank of viscount but, as this was the honour bestowed upon Jervis, his senior, after the Battle of Cape St Vincent, perhaps it was not considered entirely appropriate. Back in England the newspapers that had so criticised him now praised him to the skies. Bonfires were lit across the country, children were given holidays from school and there was a huge demand for souvenirs and commemoratives. Many new songs were penned and there were even two new dances that became fashionable – the 'Vanguard' and 'the Breaking of the Line'. Nelson received many letters including the following ecstatic note from Emma Hamilton:

'I am delirious with joy and assure you I have a fever caused by agitation and pleasure. Good God what a victory! Never, never has there been anything half so glorious, half so complete... I fainted when I heard the joyful news and fell on my side and am hurt, but what of that I should feel it a glory to die in such a cause. No I would not like to die until I see and embrace the *Victor of the Nile*... My dress from head to foot is *alla Nelson*. Even my shawl is in blue with gold anchors all over. My earrings are Nelson's anchors; in short we are all be-Nelsoned...'

Lady Hamilton

When Nelson arrived in Naples, the King and Queen as well as the Hamiltons rowed out to meet him, accompanied by an orchestra playing *See the Conquering Hero Comes*. Hundreds of birds were released from cages on the shore and he was offered accommodation with the Hamiltons. Emma was making elaborate plans to celebrate his fortieth birthday. He wrote to Fanny that, 'The preparations of Lady Hamilton for celebrating my birthday are enough to fill me with vanity. Every ribbon, every button has *Nelson* etc, and the whole service are "*H.N. Glorious 1st August!*" Songs and sonnets are numerous, beyond what I could ever deserve.'

It was a huge celebration – 80 came to dinner at Sir William's, 800 to supper and 1,740 came to the ball. Josiah Nisbet had to be taken out, drunk, by Captain Troubridge because he was complaining of his stepfather's attentions to Lady Hamilton. In truth, Josiah was not popular in the navy, many feeling his captaincy unwarranted and solely due to Nelson's influence. However, he would not be the last to find Nelson's behaviour towards Lady Hamilton unseemly.

Emma Hamilton was born Emily Lyon in 1765, the

daughter of a blacksmith in the Wirral. She became a nursery maid at a young age, first working close to home and then moving to London to take up another position in domestic service. She worked in the musical household of Thomas Linley. Linley's second son was a midshipman who was nursed by Emma when he came back home extremely ill with a fever. By the age of 14, she was employed by a Mrs Kelly, the madam of a brothel in Arlington Street. It is possible that she entered the household only as a servant but she did not stay as such for very long. Emma became the mistress of a naval officer, Captain John Willet Payne, a good friend of the Prince of Wales. It is also claimed that she was an attendant at the Temple of Health and Hymen, and that she posed for artists at the Royal Academy but there is not enough surviving evidence to be certain. Aged 16, she moved to a cottage near Uppark in Sussex as the mistress of Sir Harry Featherstonhaugh to whom she bore a child, named Emma, who was left with her grandmother. Around this time she first sat for the artist George Romney who would later paint her many times and in various guises. While still in Sussex she met Charles Greville who became her protector in London when the affair with Sir Harry ended. At this point she changed her name to 'Emma Hart'. The arrangement with Greville ended when he became engaged to an heiress but he was concerned for Emma's future and wrote to his uncle Sir William Hamilton. Hamilton's wife had died in 1782 and he agreed to look after Emma. So, in 1786, she left England with her mother to join him in Naples. For some time she was very unhappy without Greville, whom she had been falsely led to believe would return for her. William Hamilton did his best to cheer her up and make her welcome, buying her clothes and taking her to the theatre. She had no thoughts of a closer relationship, declaring that he would never be her lover, although she liked him very much. In his turn, William was very much attracted to her. She spent her time in Naples as the hostess for Sir William's formal dinner parties, and William paid for her to take language, music and singing lessons, and to attend the opera. He also encouraged every painter in Naples to take her likeness. She was undoubtedly a great beauty and she caught the eye of the King, Ferdinand IV. However, although Emma was gratified and excited by the King's attention to her, he had too much respect for Sir William to make advances to his protegé. Perhaps this was the reason Emma was also able to become good friends with Queen Maria Carolina, who had been known to banish other women who had been close to the King. It was around this period that Emma began to entertain invited guests with her celebrated 'attitudes' – in which she posed as Greek and Roman figures. Once she finally accepted that her relationship with

Greville was finished, she allowed herself to succumb to the kindness of Sir William and she moved into his lodgings. They married in England in 1791.

Sir William Hamilton, 35 years Emma's senior, was born in 1730. He was an intellectual whose studies on volcanoes were published in the *Philosophical Transactions of the Royal Society*. He was also a great collector of Greek and Roman antiquities, creating his own museum. When his collection was sold to the British Museum in 1772, it formed the basis of the Museum's Greek and Roman collections. Hamilton was also a man of great energy, with a taste for dancing and outdoor pursuits and was well known as a generous host. He had started his career as an officer in the army and became equerry to George III when he was the Prince of Wales. He was made a captain two years later and took part in the Seven Years War against the French. He resigned his commission around the time of his marriage to Catherine Barlow in 1758 and went into the House of Commons as MP for the pocket borough of Midhurst in Sussex. He went to Naples in 1764 to take up the position of Envoy Extraordinary and Minister Plenipotentiary to the kingdom of Naples and Sicily (also known as the Two Sicilies). At the time Naples was, after Paris, the second largest city in Europe. Hamilton quickly formed a close friendship with King Ferdinand IV that was to last many years. Emma Hart first came into

Hamilton's life when he visited his nephew Charles Greville in England in 1784 and was encouraged to take her back to Naples. As we have seen, she became his mistress in 1786, after she had been in Italy for about eight months.

From the moment of his arrival back in Naples, Nelson was drawn to Emma, or rather enchanted by her. He had never met anyone quite like her and, although she was approaching middle age and had put on weight, she was still very beautiful. Her reaction to Nelson's victory could not have been more different to Fanny's, as expressed in a letter he received:

'The newspapers have tormented and almost killed me in regard to the desperate action you have fought with the French fleet. How human faculties can be brought to make others intentionally miserable I cannot conceive. In my opinion a news paper writer or a fabricator for them is a despicable creature bearing a human shape. I trust in God for a continuance of his protection over you and to grant my dear husband a happy return to me and our good father, who has exerted his spirits very well.'

Even when Fanny knew the outcome of the battle, she was unable to share in his joy, or conceive of the Europe-wide importance of the battle. She was consumed with domestic matters and the running of Roundwood. Her constant worrying must have worn Nelson down, especially when they spent so much

time apart. Emma was carefree and vivacious and, surrounded by admiration and adoration in Naples, it was
little wonder that Nelson began to fall in love with
her. Although he did not seem to have any intention of
leaving Fanny, continuing to write to her regularly, his
letters made constant reference to Emma:

'I hope one day to have the pleasure of introducing
you to Lady Hamilton. She is one of the very best
women in this world. How few could have made the
turn she has. She is an honour to her sex and a proof
that even reputation may be regained, but I own it requires a great soul. Her kindness, with Sir William, to
me is more than I can express, I am in their house, and
I may now tell you it requires all the kindness of my
friends to set me up. Her ladyship, if Josiah was to
stay, would make something of him, and with all his
bluntness I am sure he likes Lady Hamilton more than
any female. She would fashion him in six months in
spite of himself. I believe Lady Hamilton intends writing to you.'

It was hardly a tactful letter to send to Josiah's
mother. Nelson seemed to have to write about Emma
to everyone. In a letter to St Vincent he wrote that, 'I
am writing opposite Lady Hamilton, therefore you
will not be surprised at the glorious jumble of this letter. Were your lordship in my place, I much doubt if
you could write so well: our hearts and hands must be
all in a flutter: Naples is a dangerous place and we

must keep clear of it.' Both at home and professionally his relationship with Emma was causing anxiety.

Nelson in Naples

Nelson was to stay in Naples for another eighteen months, since he was given command of naval operations east of Corsica and Sardinia. This included blockading the French in Malta and Egypt and he sent out small squadrons but he himself managed command onshore and made only a few outings to sea. In Naples, King Ferdinand was vulnerable to invasion – the French had taken Rome, removed the Pope and set up a republic. Ferdinand had an army ready to march on Rome but this meant that he would have to surrender neutrality. Nelson's presence was an extremely valuable asset to the Neapolitans since his ships could provide support to their army. Nelson, not surprisingly, was all for attack and Sir William was also urging Ferdinand to join the allied countries of Britain, Austria and Russia. They finally came to an agreement and an Austrian general arrived to lead the army while Nelson arranged for troops to be landed at Leghorn to cut the French lines. The campaign was initially successful. In November 1798, Rome was occupied by the Neapolitans and the Pope was invited to return. The French, however, called for reinforcements and, by December, they had managed to invade Neapolitan land, forcing Nelson to evacuate the royal family and the Hamiltons to Palermo.

They arrived on Boxing Day 1798 after a stormy voyage that had claimed the life of a six-year-old prince who died in the arms of Emma. Nelson again lived with the Hamiltons and he became sexually involved with Emma early in the New Year, despite being plagued by ill health. He was still suffering from migraines as well as digestive problems and pains in his chest. The change in his relationship with Emma was reflected by a change in his letters to Fanny. He made excuses for not writing to her so often and also put her off any attempt to visit him:

'You must not think it possible for me to write even to you as much as I used to. I have such quantities of writing public letters that my private correspondence, has been and must continue to be, greatly neglected. You would by February have seen how unpleasant it would have been had you followed any advice, which carried you from England to a wandering sailor... Nothing but the situation of the country has kept me from England; and if I have the happiness of seeing their Sicilian majesties safe on their throne again, it is probable I shall yet be home in the summer...'

He seemed to think of the restoration of the King and Queen as his personal mission. In April 1799, when 25 French ships escaped from Brest and were at large in the Mediterranean, and Lord Keith called for reinforcements to pursue them, Nelson sent ten ships but refused to leave Palermo himself. He wrote to St Vincent that, 'You may depend on my exertion and I am only sorry that I cannot move to your help: but this island appears to hang on my stay. Nothing could console the Queen this night but my promise not to leave them unless the battle was to be fought off Sardinia.'

It was a genuine dilemma for Nelson but he was also under the kind of influence that most affected his military judgement – the flattery of people in high places, not to mention the charms of Lady Hamilton. St Vincent was a little more sympathetic since Nelson was usefully placed in covering routes to Malta, Egypt and, of course, Sicily. Meanwhile civil war broke out in Naples. King Ferdinand had appointed a senior churchman, Cardinal Ruffo, to lead resistance against the French invasion, and he now needed reinforcements. Nelson sent four ships to his aid and, under pressure from the Queen and Emma, decided to go himself, taking both the Hamiltons with him. Naples was in chaos and Ruffo's men were meting out punishments to intellectuals and others whom they accused of sympathising with the French. To alleviate the situation Ruffo was prepared to agree to an armistice and to the surrender of the French troops but Nelson did not agree with the terms because they had not been sanctioned by the King. The result was another outbreak of violence. Nelson supplied arms to those who said that they supported Ruffo and sent marines ashore. The French were finally overcome but a series of reprisals and revenge attacks was initiated, including the hanging of the head of the Neapolitan navy whom Nelson had insisted should be court-martialled. A period of ugly repression ensued.

Between Duty and Desire

Loitering in Palermo

Lord Keith had been made commander-in-chief in the Mediterranean and again needed reinforcements as Minorca was in danger from the French – and he wanted Nelson to take command in defending it. It was an important strategic base for Britain in blockading Toulon. Only upon Keith's third request did Nelson reluctantly send out four ships but he refused to leave Naples himself, believing his duty to lie with the royal family and that this was more important to him than the potential loss of Minorca. It was flagrant insubordination but he was 'prepared for any fate which may await my disobedience'. However, in 1799, when Keith was pursuing the French and Spanish fleets through the Straits of Gibraltar, Nelson was left in charge of the Mediterranean fleet. Ferdinand rewarded Nelson's loyalty with the dukedom of Bronte in Sicily. They all returned to Palermo where relations with the Hamiltons were becoming difficult. Sir William was tired of the heavy expenses in entertaining naval visitors and was also aware of the ever closer relationship between his wife and Nelson.

When Lord Keith returned to the Mediterranean early in 1800 he insisted on meeting Nelson at Leghorn and accompanying him back to Palermo. Unsurprisingly, it was not a pleasant visit. Keith wrote of it, 'The whole was a scene of fulsome Vanity and Absurdity all the long eight days. I was sick of Palermo and its allurements...' His view of Nelson and Emma was that they were 'just a silly pair of sentimental fools,' and Nelson was 'cutting the most absurd figure possible for folly and vanity.'

Keith took Nelson with him to join the fleet blockading Malta which was occupied by the French. On board the *Foudroyant* on 18 February 1800, the French vessel *Le Genereux* from Aboukir Bay was sighted and Nelson ordered them to give chase. A battle ensued and, with the British doggedly firing at the masts and the yards of the enemy, the mortally wounded French admiral was forced into surrender. In his despatches Keith gave Nelson full credit for the action but it was not long before Nelson crossed him again. Keith wanted Nelson to remain in charge of the Malta blockade while he went to Genoa. Again Nelson refused him, this time on the grounds of his health, and insisted on returning to his friends in Palermo.

It was a matter of great concern to two of Nelson's most loyal captains, Hardy and Troubridge. Troubridge had tried to appeal to him before, warning

Nelson of the mounting gossip: 'If you knew what your friends feel for you I am sure that you would cut out all the nocturnal parties; the gambling of the people at Palermo is talked of everywhere. I beseech your Lordship, leave off. Lady H——'s character will suffer; nothing can prevent people from talking; a Gambling Woman in the eyes of an Englishman is lost.' He also wrote directly to Lady Hamilton, warning her 'of the ideas that were going about. You may not know that you have many enemies. I therefore risk your displeasure by telling you…'

However nothing it seemed would stop the two lovers. Nelson resigned his command and received a letter from Lord Spencer, the First Lord of the Admiralty: 'It is by no means my wish to call you away from service, but having observed that you have been under the necessity of quitting your station off Malta, on account of the state of your health, which I am persuaded you could not have thought of doing without such necessity, it appeared to me much more advisable to come home at once than to be obliged to remain inactive at Palermo…'

Return to England

Despite the politeness, it was really an order to return. Since it was also the intention of the Hamiltons to return to England, Nelson decided to go. He was not excited by the prospect of return so one has to wonder what he would have done if it were not for the fact that Emma would be with him. By this point she was pregnant by Nelson, a fact to which Sir William had decided to turn a blind eye. Keith would not allow them to use a warship for the entire journey and, in any case, at Leghorn, Emma, suffering from morning sickness, decided that she was unable to bear the trials of a sea voyage. The journey overland could not be direct because they had to avoid the areas occupied by the French. They travelled via Florence, Trieste, Klagenfurt, Vienna, Prague, a barge down the Elbe, Dresden and then Hamburg. They expected a navy frigate would pick them up from Hamburg but one was not forthcoming and they took a packet boat heading for Great Yarmouth. The journey was punctuated throughout by local celebrations in Nelson's honour. Witnesses to their travels made plenty of comments about the couple and neither came off very well. However, other than comments upon Nelson's appearance, vanity and attention to Emma, the real animosity was reserved for her.

Lord Malmesbury's son remarked in Vienna that to see them together was 'really disgusting' and that she was 'without exception the most coarse, ill-mannered, disagreeable woman'. Austrian Franz Cullenbrach wrote that 'Lady Hamilton never stopped talking, singing, laughing, gesticulating and mimicking while the favoured son of Neptune appeared to leave her no more than did her shadow, trying to meet with his own small eyes, the great orbs of his beloved, and, withal, as motionless and silent as a monument, embarrassed by his poor figure and by all the emblems, cords and crosses with which he was bedecked.' The news had not escaped the English newspapers, and they were no longer heaping praise upon him. A report in the *Morning Chronicle* said that, 'There is indeed a terrible scene to be unfolded of what has passed in Naples these last twelve months. We can assert from the best information, that the British name has suffered a reproach on the Continent by the transaction at Naples.' Another journalist, commenting on a German painter working on a portrait of Nelson and Emma, wrote that, 'An Irish correspondent hopes the artist will have delicacy enough to put Sir William *between* them.' Well-known caricaturists of the day such as Gillray and Rowlandson all published satires of Nelson and his mistress.

End of a Marriage

The party arrived in England on 6 November and, a few days later, Nelson met Fanny at a hotel in London. It was a difficult and inevitably strained meeting – the Hamiltons were around and Nelson's father had also come to meet him. Of course, Fanny was aware of all the reports that were circulating and it must have been a humiliating experience for her. They had not seen each other in three years and Nelson's letters had become less frequent, especially during the time his relationship with Lady Hamilton had intensified. Before meeting Emma he had seemed content with his marriage, even if her sometimes inefficient housekeeping had irritated him and her reserved nature was alien to his own. Perhaps, too, the fact that they had not had children had been a disappointment and, with Lady Hamilton pregnant, this must have been even more soul-destroying for Fanny. Nelson started to ignore Fanny more and more, though she appears to have acted with dignity throughout, at least in public. Lady Spencer wrote that he 'treated her with every mark of dislike and even of contempt'. He invited the Hamiltons to dine with them and insensitively proposed that Fanny should help Emma who was suffering nausea with the pregnancy. Unsurprisingly, the party broke up.

While many in polite society, including the King, now shunned Nelson and, more particularly, Lady Hamilton, his popularity with the general public remained high and he continued to be feted wherever he went, including at a huge reception in Great Yarmouth. He was cheered at the theatre in London and, when he attended the Lord Mayor's Banquet, it was the crowd who pulled his coach up Ludgate Hill.

The crowd enjoyed the decorations he wore which society found vain and pretentious. But the real reason, of course, for his popularity was his success against the French. The fear of invasion was a day-to-day reality for people at the time and cannot be underestimated.

The Christmas of 1800 marked the irretrievable breakdown of Nelson's marriage. Together with the Hamiltons, Nelson was invited to spend the festive season with William Beckford at Fonthill in Wiltshire and Fanny was not invited. Beckford was a very rich eccentric who was at the edges of society and he offered Nelson, 'a few comfortable days of repose – uncontaminated by the sight of drawing-room parasites' – in other words, without the 'respectable' families of the Wiltshire set. After Christmas, Nelson did go home briefly to Fanny but left after they quarrelled – inevitably over Lady Hamilton. After they parted, following what would turn out to be the last occasion on which they saw each other, Nelson went to Plymouth to take command of the *San Josef*, one of the ships captured at St Vincent. He sent Fanny a brief but cordial note: 'My dear Fanny, We are arrived, and heartily tired; and with kindest regards to my father, believe me, your affectionate Nelson.' He arranged for a quarterly allowance to be paid into her account and, although Roundwood had been sold, he had taken another house for a year where she would remain.

It was a difficult time for Nelson and he was depressed – although most of his troubles he had, of course, brought upon himself. He was compromised both personally and professionally. He was now separated from those he loved and even St Vincent felt that, in his current state, he was unfit to lead a fleet. Lord Keith, who had never had a great deal of affection for him, felt the same way. St Vincent's attitude would have a significant bearing on Nelson's future postings when he became the First Lord in February 1801. Nelson, with his uncompromising and virtually suicidal fighting style, was recognised as a massive deterrent to enemy fleets. However, while he persisted in his contact with Lady Hamilton, his personal needs were to be repeatedly ignored, and he would be kept at sea for as long as the war went on.

At the time of their separation Emma was about to give birth to their child. He was desperate to be with her alone and to sleep with her: 'It sets me on fire, even the thoughts, much more would be the reality. I am sure my love and desires are all to you and if any woman were to come to me, even as I am this moment from thinking of you, I hope it might rot off if I would touch her even with my hand. No, my heart, my person and mind is in perfect union of love towards my own, dear beloved Emma… My own dear wife, for such you are in my eyes and in the face of heaven…' They feared such intimate letters would be intercepted and made public and would allow only Sir

William's secretary to bring letters to and from Nelson's ship. As a further safeguard they invented two characters – a seaman on board Nelson's ship and his lover who was also a friend of Emma's, calling them the Thompsons – and Nelson would write sometimes as many as four letters a day. Although he was miserable at being alone and was suffering with his eye again, he was ecstatic at the news that he had a baby daughter born on 1 February.

'I believe poor dear Mrs Thompson's friend will go mad with joy. He cries, prays, and performs all tricks, yet dare not show all or any of his feelings, but he has only me to consult with. He swears he will drink your health this day in a bumper, and damn me if I don't join him in spite of all the doctors in Europe, [he had been advised not to drink alcohol on account of the eye] for none regard you with truer affection than myself. You are a dear, good creature and your kindness and attentions to poor Mrs T stamps you higher than ever in my mind. I cannot write, I am so agitated by this young man at my elbow. I believe he is foolish; he does nothing but rave about you and her. I own I participate of his joy and cannot write anything.'

Nelson wanted the child to be named Emma, not being aware that Lady Hamilton already had a daughter of the same name who was now twenty-one years old. So the name that was settled upon was Horatia. The child was found a nurse, a Mrs Gibson, and went to live with her in Little Titchfield Street in London. Sir William's extraordinary tolerance of the affair would not extend to having the child brought up in his house and Emma's lifestyle, which she showed no signs of wanting to change, was not conducive to raising a child. Nelson rushed to London when he had the opportunity of three days' leave before he changed ship in readiness for joining operations in the Baltic. He arrived in London before dawn and went to see his daughter for the first time with Emma. He wrote that, 'a finer child was never produced by any two persons. It was in truth a love-begotten child.'

Fanny wanted to come to London to talk to Nelson but he put her off, saying that he was on very particular business, and also warned her not to come to Portsmouth as he was never on shore. This delighted Lady Hamilton who wrote to her new-found friend Sarah Nelson (Nelson's sister-in-law, wife to his brother William) that, 'She offered to go down but was refused. She only wanted to do mischief to all the great JOVE's relations. 'Tis now shewn, all her ill-treatment and bad-heart — JOVE has found it out.' Nelson wrote Fanny another letter before departing making it absolutely clear that he wanted nothing more to do with her or her son, for whom he felt he had done as much as he could: 'But I have done my duty as an honest, generous man, and I neither want or wish for anybody to care what becomes of me, whether I return or am left in the Baltic. Living I have done all in my power for you, and if dead, you will only find I have done the same; therefore my only wish is to be left to myself; and wishing you every happiness, Believe that I am, Your affectionate Nelson.'

Fanny marked the top of the letter: 'This is my Lord Nelson's letter of dismissal, which so astonished me that I immediately sent it to Mr Maurice Suckling, who was sincerely attached to me, for his advice; he desired me not to take the least notice of it as his Brother seemed to have forgot himself.' She wrote to Nelson several times to beg him to reconsider. He did not reply. The last of her letters was returned with what have must been a truly hurtful note by one of Nelson's friends, 'Opened by mistake by Lord Nelson, but not read.'

Copenhagen

March saw Nelson finally back at sea under Admiral Sir Hyde Parker and together they headed into the Baltic. Their aim was to provoke the Danish into pulling out of a pact called 'The Neutrality of the North'. This had been set up to try and protect the Baltic states' trade links with France from the British. Parker was under orders to take the drastic action of destroying the Danish fleet if they refused to withdraw from the pact. Near Copenhagen, Hyde Parker planned to blockade the Baltic but the problem with this strategy was that it would give the Baltic states time to prepare as well as to consolidate their combined navies. Nelson proposed immediate attack on the Danish ships at anchor in King's Deep in front of the city of Copenhagen and Parker agreed. Nelson transferred to the 74 gun *Elephant* which had a shallower draft than his ship and hence was more suitable for the waters that they were in.

On 2 April 1801, the British prepared for battle as the wind became favourable to them. The battle had been going on for about two hours when two British ships flagged distress signals and Admiral Parker replied by making the signal to withdraw. Nelson was furious and disobeyed the order, putting the telescope to his blind eye and saying to the captain, 'You know Foley, I have only one eye – I have the right to be blind sometimes. I really do not see the signal.' (Contrary to popular belief, he did not hold the telescope to his blind eye and say 'I see no ships'.)

After three hours, despite the damage that they had sustained, the Danes continued to fight back so Nelson issued an ultimatum: 'If the firing is continued on the part of Denmark, Lord Nelson will be obliged to set on fire all the floating batteries he has taken without the power of saving the brave Danes who have defended them.' The Danes backed down and onshore the following day Nelson again took up the position of a diplomat for Britain and brokered a 14-week armistice. The successful campaign went some way to re-establishing Nelson's reputation, especially when Hyde Parker was called back to England because of his lack of action and undue caution towards the enemy. Nelson paraded his fleet warningly past the Swedish and Russian naval bases and the neutrality pact all but collapsed. When the news arrived that Tsar Paul I of Russia, one of its primary instigators, had been assassinated, it was more or less finished off.

At Home with Emma

In June, Nelson returned home to the welcome news that he had been made a viscount. His first stop after arriving at Great Yarmouth in July was the hospital where naval casualties were being treated and then he dashed to London and to Emma. With the danger of French invasion still high he was not at leisure to spend as much time with Emma and his daughter as he may have wished although he was now to be stationed close to home. On 26 July, he was placed in command of a counter-invasion force to protect the Thames, the Medway and the coastlines of Kent, Sussex and Essex, ranging from Beachy Head to Orford Ness. Nelson based himself in Deal in Kent from where he could oversee operations. Immediately, he looked for opportunities to go on the offensive rather than wait for the enemy and on 15 August he planned to attack the French barges, gathered for a potential invasion, which were anchored in Boulogne. The French, however, expected the British and were well prepared. Their ships were positioned across the mouth of the harbour with chain cables, nets were put over the vessels to prevent the enemy from boarding them and each crew included troops as well as seamen. For the British it was a disastrous attempt, not helped by the current which carried them past their targets. The failure left 45 British dead and 128 injured, among them two of Nelson's closest colleagues, Captain Edward Parker and Lieutenant Frederick Langford. Nelson was in very low spirits and devastated when Parker died of his wounds. He wanted leave but the Admiralty, continuing to frustrate him even when it was a matter of his health, refused it.

He revived when Emma wrote that, as he had asked, she had found him a house, situated in Merton, Surrey. Nelson was excited by the plans that Emma had for the place. Not only did she have considerable talent at creating a home but he also hoped that Horatia would be able to live at Merton at least some of the time. With Sir William also resident it was still not possible for Horatia to be there permanently, although he and Nelson remained remarkably good friends. Sir William wrote to him:

'We have now inhabited your Lordship's property for some days and I can now speak with some certainty. I have lived with our dear Emma some several years. I know her merits, and have an opinion of the head and heart that God Almighty has been pleased to give her; but a seaman alone could have given a fine woman full power to chuse and fit up a residence without seeing it himself. You are in luck, for, on my conscience, I verily believe that a place so suitable to your views could not have been found at so cheap a rate...You have nothing but to come and enjoy it immediately... It would make you laugh to see Emma and her mother fitting up pig-sties and hen coops and already the canal is enlivened with ducks and the cock is strutting with his hens along thc walks. Your Lordship's plan as to stocking the Canal is exactly mine. I will answer for it, that in a few months you may command a good dish of fish at a moment's warning.'

In 1801, peace negotiations were underway with France. The peace would not last more than two years, but it gave Nelson the welcome opportunity to see his house for the first time and to remain there until 1803. The house was virtually a shrine to Nelson. His friend Lord Minto wrote after he visited in 1802:

'She [Lady Hamilton] goes on cramming Nelson with trowelfuls of flattery, which he goes on taking as quietly as a child does pap. The love she makes to him is not only ridiculous, but disgusting: not only the rooms but the whole house, staircases and all, are covered with nothing but pictures of her and him, of all sizes and all sorts, and representations of his naval actions, coats of arms, pieces of plate in his honour, the flagstaff of 'L'Orient' etc. — an excess of vanity which counteracts its own purpose. If it was Lady H's house there might be a pretence for it; to make his own a mere looking-glass to view himself all day is in bad taste.'

Sir William too found the whole place rather overwhelming, writing to Emma that, 'I have no complaint to make but I feel the whole attention of my wife is given to Ld N. and his interest at Merton. I well know the purity of Ld N's friendship for Emma and me, and I know how very uncomfortable it would make his Lp, our best friend, if a separation should take place, & am therefore determined to do all in my power to prevent such an extremity, which would be essentially detrimental to all parties, but would be more sensibly felt by our dear friend than by us.'

He was determined not to rock the boat and not to argue with Emma for the sake of everyone's happiness and, no doubt, for a quiet life. As for Nelson, he had never been happier. His father died in April 1802 but not before he had enjoyed a visit to Merton. However, the old man's sympathies had really lain with Fanny.

Nelson did not attend the funeral because he did not want to meet his wife, a decision in which he must have been heavily influenced by Emma. Despite his loss, this was a period of domestic bliss and comfort for Nelson, of a kind that he had never really known. In the summer of 1802, Nelson and the Hamiltons went on a tour of the West Country and South Wales and again Nelson was greeted with cheering and adoring crowds wherever he went. There were still problems in polite society. The party was snubbed by the Duke of Marlborough at Blenheim but, amongst so much gaiety, this cannot have seemed very important. Apart from this onc trip, they stayed at Merton. The trio was broken up by the death of Sir William on 6 April 1803; he was in Emma's arms when he died while Nelson held his hand. For form's sake Nelson went to lodgings in London.

France declared war on Britain again in May, as had been expected, and on 14 May Nelson was given an appointment by the Admiralty to the *Victory*, which was lying in Portsmouth docks. He arrived on 20 May and wrote to Emma almost as soon as he boarded:

'You will believe that although I am glad to leave that horrid place, Portsmouth, yet being afloat makes me now feel that we do not tread the same element. I feel from my soul God is good, and His due wisdom will unite us, only when you look upon our dear child call to your remembrance all you think I would say was I present, and be assured that I am thinking of you every moment. My heart is full to bursting! May God Almighty bless & protect you, is the fervent prayer of, my dear beloved Emma, your most faithful, affectionate Nelson & Bronte.'

He was also much concerned for Horatia, hoping that she might come to live at Merton full time now that Sir William was no longer there. Previously, Nelson had had the opportunities of seeing her there but only when William was away. Before going to Portsmouth he also joined Emma to christen their now two-year-old daughter 'Horatia Nelson Thompson' in Marylebone.

He wrote many letters from the ship, thanking Emma for taking care of his child and offering advice such as putting nets over the canal in case the little one fell in. However, the truth was that Emma was seeing less of Horatia than before, claiming that the nurse, Mrs Gibson, was reluctant to give her up. In fact, she never showed any real inclination to install Horatia at Merton. For the moment, Nelson had to turn the focus of his attention to war.

HMS Victory and Life on Board Ship

The Building of Victory

The order for a new ship was decided upon in 1759, when Nelson was one year old, and the ship was to become *HMS Victory*. 1759 was also the year that Watt invented the steam engine with a separate condenser which would eventually lead to the abandonment of sailing vessels. The warrant to build *Victory* went to Mr Edward Allen, the master shipwright at Chatham Dockyard in Kent. The Navy's senior surveyor, Thomas Slade, was the designer and the cost of building the ship was £63,176, an enormous sum. The name Victory was one of a possible seven decided by the Admiralty and may have been finally chosen because 1759 was an Annus Mirabilis, a year of victories, for the Navy. There were doubts about the name, however, since the previous vessel that had borne it had been lost with all hands.

It was a long process to get *Victory* to sea. The design would have first been worked out on paper, and a model built. Next the keel would be laid, and to this would be fixed oak timbers like ribs — the first at the front and then the stern-post that would take the rudder. The midship floor would be installed as well as the rest of the framework. The ribs would be planked on both sides, and the beams laid across for the decks. When this was complete bulkheads were used to divide up the rooms and cabins inside. Finally the bottom of the ship was coppered, although *Victory* was not coppered until 1780 when she was refitted according to a new Navy Board directive. As well as providing protection against the teredo (a sea worm that could bore through wood) this also improved her speed capacity. *Victory* turned out to be a ship that handled very well and she could reach speeds of up to 11 knots (12 miles per hour), though that was under excellent conditions. More likely she would travel at around 8 knots.

Victory required around 6000 trees, the majority of them oak. This equates to approximately 100 acres of woodland. The timber that was used was well seasoned, having been stored for fourteen years with the express purpose of building a first rate ship, and this contributed to her longevity. The bottom of the ship was protected by 3,923 copper sheets, each 4ft by 14 inches. Initially there were around 250 men working on building the ship but her completion became less urgent as the Seven Years War ended and the workforce was reduced.

Once she was complete there was still the need for

sails, masts, anchors and ropes. *Victory* could carry 37 sails and had 23 spare on board, making an astonishing total area of 6,510 square yards of canvas. To rig the sails 26 miles of cordage was needed. She had seven anchors, the heaviest weighing 4.51 tonnes. Anchors of different weights were required for different circumstances. For example, in shallow waters, a lighter anchor was the most effective.

Victory was a 'first rate ship'. The Navy had six rates of ship at this time and the rating was based essentially on the number of guns that the ship could carry. A first rate ship like the *Victory* would have 100 to 112 guns and a crew of up to 841. The smallest sixth rate ships had 20 guns and a crew of 138. A first rate was also referred to as a 'ship of the line' (as were other rates that had 60 guns or more) because it was only a ship with that capacity that could stand in the line of battle when they went into action.

At the Battle of Trafalgar *Victory* was armed as follows:

Lower gun deck 30 x 32 pounders
Middle gun deck 28 x 24 pounders
Upper gun deck 30 x 12 long pounders
Quarter gun deck 12 x12 short pounders
Forecastle 2 x 12 medium pounders
2 x 68 pounders carronade

The guns were named after the weight of the shot that they fired. Generally round shot was used but, at close range, they might also use grape shot. This was a bag filled with many small balls that would create havoc on the enemy's deck. In addition there was chain shot designed to cut up rigging which would also be used only at short range.

The Geography of a Ship

First rate vessels were all structured in a similar way in terms of the number of decks. At the very bottom of the ship was the hold filled with ballast. It was also the storage area for a huge number of casks of fresh water, salt pork and beef — there needed to be enough to feed 800 men over a six-month period. In addition, there would be the powder magazine room, lined with a cloth to keep it waterproof, and a tin-lined room for storing bread. The hold would invariably be the home to a large number of rats, and would be very dark and smell strongly of bilge water. The rats broke into food casks and were even capable of gnawing through the sides of a ship. In times of short rations on long voyages they were sometimes eaten by the sailors who called them 'millers' because they would often be covered in flour dust.

The next deck up was near the waterline and known as the orlop deck. It housed the cabins for jun-

ior officers and the cockpit which was both the accommodation for older midshipmen and the place
where the wounded would be treated during a battle.
The fore-cockpit was home to the boatswain and the
carpenter. Stored on the orlop were spare sail and the
cable tiers.

The lower deck was where the majority of the crew
ate and slept. It also held the heaviest tier of guns in
two rows on either side of the vessel. The gun room
was situated here with sleeping quarters for the gunner and junior midshipmen. At the front was the
manger compartment which fulfilled two functions. It
was designed to prevent water that came through the
hawses from washing across the deck and was also the
place where livestock was kept.

The middle deck was filled with more rows of guns
and above was the upper deck, also called the main
deck, with additional guns. The ward room was situated here where the senior officers messed and their
accommodation led off from it. Higher than these the
quarterdeck, where only senior officers could walk,
ran from the stern to the main mast and was linked by
gangways to the forecastle on the same level. The poop
deck was situated above the quarterdeck and was the
roof of the captain's cabin. The captain's cabin would
also open out to a stern gallery where he would be
able to find a little peace to walk on his own.

Victory's History

The keel was laid down in July 1759 but it would not be until 1776 that *Victory* was commissioned by the Admiralty and she was fitted out, and not until 1778 that her first commander, Sir John Lindsay, took her to sea. When Nelson joined his first ship in 1771 he would have been able to see the *Victory* moored up. At the time she was under repair as the bottom boards were loose and she was in some danger of sinking. She would stay there for another five years. Before Nelson finally became her captain, *Victory* had quite a history and had undergone various changes in repairs and increasing her firing power, as well as having had an illustrious list of admirals in command of her. She saw service in the American War of Independence as the flagship of Admiral Keppel. In 1781, under Admiral Kempenfelt, she captured an entire convoy of ships that were being escorted by the French from Brest to the West Indies. The following year, this time with Admiral Howe in command, she was in action off Cape Spartel and in relieving Gibraltar. She was then back in England in 1793 for a refit which cost £15,372. Almost immediately she was required again as the French Revolutionary war began and she became the flagship of Lord Hood. Another refit was needed in Chatham in 1795, before a return to the Mediterranean theatre for an unsuccessful action in which Admiral Hotham was unable to engage the French, and the British fleet had to withdraw. This time Nelson was in the arena in command of the *Agamemnon*. Nelson was instrumental in the British success at *Victory's* next battle at Cape St Vincent, under Jervis.

Nelson almost lost the chance to command *Victory* because, when she returned to Portsmouth, a survey condemned her. She was 32-years-old by then and the intention was to convert her into a hospital ship. However, she was reprieved when another first rate vessel, *Impregnable*, was sunk in October 1799, leaving the Navy short of a ship of the line. *Victory* was then given extensive repairs and some modernisation. Two extra gun ports were added, the magazines lined with copper, the stern gallery closed in, and a simpler figurehead replaced the older one. The masts had originally been made from a single tree trunk, but now were replaced with pole masts that were made of several trunks bound together with iron hoops. She also was given a new livery — the black and yellow that were familiar at Trafalgar — except that the port hatches were painted black to make the 'Nelson chequer' which was to become standard after the battle. The next chapter will deal in depth with the following part of *Victory's* history when she was captained by Thomas Hardy and was, of course, Nelson's flagship at the Battle of Trafalgar.

The Life of the Crew

Before examining the battle itself, we will look at the life on board and the day-to-day running of a first rate ship. At Trafalgar the crew of *Victory* was made up of 820 men, with 146 Royal Marines of the Chatham Division under the command of Captain Charles Adair, 9 commissioned officers, 21 midshipmen, 77 warrant and petty officers with the rest comprised of ordinary seamen, able seamen and 31 boys. 700 were from the British Isles and the rest from 18 other nationalities including Dutch, West Indian, African, Italian, Brazilian, Maltese and even French. The mix of nationalities was not at all uncommon; they may have been taken by a press gang but were more likely to be volunteers. Usually they would be from neutral countries. To have French sailors aboard was more unusual but by no means unprecedented.

The boys on board ship were officially 13 years old (except for officers' sons who could be eleven) but fairly often they were younger. Boys aged seven were not unheard of. The youngest on board *Victory* at the Battle of Trafalgar, however, was 12-year-old Thomas Twitchen. They performed menial tasks and they could be rated as servants to the wardroom. The next lowest ratings were the landsmen or idlers who had no skills in seamanship. The ordinary and able seamen formed the bulk of the crew, and during this period they did not have a uniform. (One would not be officially introduced until 1857.) However, when they went ashore they had invented their own kind of uniform which led to the name 'Jack Tar' for a sailor. It comprised a tarred black tarpaulin hat, a long ribbon with the name of their ship embroidered on it, wide cut baggy trousers of blue or white and a blue jacket. There were, of course, variations but sailors were generally a recognisable group. Gold earrings were common as well as black buckled shoes. They came from a variety of backgrounds but were mainly uneducated and often illiterate. In comparison the midshipmen were potential officers and usually they came from either families of the landed gentry (often second or third sons who would not inherit) or from respectable professional families like Nelson's.

The warrant officers differed from the other officers in that they were not commissioned by the Admiralty but held a warrant from the Navy Office. In the ship hierarchy they came below the commissioned officers. They included personnel such as the surgeon, the master, the boatswain, the gunner, the cook, the carpenter and the purser. The surgeon would be qualified in his field. At the time a surgeon was less highly qualified than a physician but the Navy had very few physicians. The master was the most senior warrant officer, responsible for navigation, and quite often was originally a midshipman who was appointed by the captain as a master's mate. This would perhaps be a midshipman who had little family influence, making it hard to proceed further up the ranks, and who therefore settled for a warrant. The purser was responsible for the ship's provisions. The victuals were supplied by the Navy and he was expected to keep account of these, and, in addition, from his own purse he was expected to supply commodities such as coal and oil for the galley. His account would be credited by the Navy for these. To the men he also supplied tobacco and clothing, or 'slops' as they were called. Sometimes he acted as a banker for the crew but, despite what the title 'purser' might suggest, he had nothing to do with paying men. The boatswain was in charge of the cables, rigging, cordage, sails and the anchors. Generally the boatswain, like the purser had to have some education in order to keep the necessary accounts and write reports. A carpenter had to be highly skilled and often spent part of his career in the dockyards and would be a qualified shipwright before getting a warrant.

Also on board there was usually a chaplain. If not, the captain would conduct services on a Sunday, some giving sermons, others simply reciting the Articles of War. It was not uncommon for a ship to carry passengers, as when Nelson escorted Lady Hughes and her daughter. Women were not as rare at sea as commonly thought, although it was usually during peacetime that they were more tolerated. Some warrant officers such as the cook and the boatswain took their wives to sea on a more or less permanent basis. They often assisted their husbands but were not registered on the ship's books and made their own arrangements with the purser for food and other supplies. There was some kind of unwritten understanding that these women were older and preferably plain, since a young nubile woman would have been too distracting. Captains were sometimes accompanied by their wives and, like other officers, sometimes took mistresses with them. It is also true that there were occasional cases of women sailors disguised as men.

As well as the rats there was likely to be a large number of other animals aboard. The Navy provided cattle and, depending on the size of the ship, there could be any number between 10 and 60 on board. In addition there were goats, chickens and pigs. The hens were kept in coops and the others in the manger but the goats generally roamed free. Chickens and pigs were usually brought by the officers as part of their private rations, or sometimes a mess group might club together to purchase one. Pets, such as dogs and ship's cats, were also tolerated to a certain extent, particularly in peacetime. If the destination of the voyage was a suitable one, it was common for men to bring back exotic birds or monkeys for their sweethearts or to sell back in England.

The officers had a little more comfort than the men but, whatever status a man had on board, life at sea was both hard and dangerous. It is often portrayed today as unbearably severe and miserable. How an individual reacted to it depended partly upon the life that the sailor was used to at home. For a poor man, living in squalid conditions, there were some attractions to joining the Navy – regular meals that were more plentiful than at home, regular employment and wages with the potential of prize money and a pension, the opportunity for medical attention. To eat meat four times a week was not possible for the majority of civilians at that time. Discipline is a subject that always comes up in discussions of life on board a ship but, as N.A.M Rodger points out in his book *The Wooden World*, the word needs to be treated with some caution. At the time, in common usage it was taken to mean 'training', in the same sense that we speak today of a 'scientific discipline'. Orders were obeyed instantly not simply because of a fear of punishment but because every sailor knew that the safety of the entire ship and crew depended on co-ordinated teamwork. In 1749 the Admiralty revised the Articles of War (the code by which it operated) to make attacks on officers onshore a matter subject to court martial. However they usually turned a blind eye to such attacks, so unpopular or harsh officers and captains were consequently vulnerable and had good reason to maintain a happy ship. Although at sea a captain had autonomy he was not entirely a law unto himself. During the Seven Years War three officers were dismissed from the service for excessive use of punishment and repression. This is not to imply that punishment was not harsh but it should be remembered that there is a difference between today's standards and those of the eighteenth century. Punishment almost invariably meant flogging, and the maximum number of strokes that a captain could inflict was 12, although fairly frequently more were given. The problem was that the Articles of War did not legislate adequately for alternatives for minor misdemeanours, and mostly dealt with procedures for infractions by officers. So punishment varied from ship to ship. A captain might resort to using a cane to give a swift blow to lazy worker, or might curtail leave or make a man responsible for cleaning the heads. A court martial for very serious offences could result in extreme punishments of between 100 and 300 lashes but many captains would try to avoid them, partly from humanity and partly because of the administrative difficulties. To hold a court martial it was necessary to be in port and to gather together the second-in-command of the port, as well as a minimum of five post captains (or, failing that, commanders) and a maximum of 13.

A Day on Board Ship

The day on board ship was divided into seven 'watches' of four hours each. The men were divided into two groups, also known as the larboard watch and the starboard watch, and they took it in turns to cover each of the seven watches. The uneven number was so that night duties were equally shared. The landsmen were not included in the watches. Men that had duties that required particularly intense concentration such as look-outs and the helmsman would change at each bell. They would still be required on duty but would be put to another task. Of course, if there was severe weather or a battle, all hands would be required on deck. Time was marked by the ringing of a bell every half an hour, so the end of a watch would be marked by eight bells. The officers were divided into three watches so they had the advantage of being able to sleep for more than four hours at a time in more comfortable quarters. The majority of the men slept on the lower gun deck in hammocks, each allocated a space of 14 inches. Usually, however, they would have double that space while the other watch was on duty. During the day the hammocks were stored in nets on the side of the main deck where they would have a chance to air and, during action, provide some protection against musket balls and even cannon, acting like sandbags.

The ship's day ran from noon to noon and the routine was essentially the same every day. Activity began between five o'clock and half past five in the morning when the idlers would start scrubbing down the deck with holy stones and the cook and his mates would light the fires in the galley to prepare the day's food. The first watch would be woken and the hammocks stowed on deck before breakfast was served at eight o'clock. The watch that was on duty would be pared down to a minimum so that as many men as possible could eat at the same time. The men messed in groups of eight on tables between the guns. Breakfast consisted of 'burgoo' which was a kind of porridge without milk and sweetened with molasses. If it was available, there would be cocoa with which to wash it down. Afterwards, the watch below would clear the lower deck and might be allowed to rest or might be told to exercise with the guns. Some days would be put aside for the washing, mending or making of clothes. Any floggings ordered by the captain would take place at eleven o'clock, either daily, if required, or on a single, designated day. All hands were summoned to witness punishment (presumably to maximise its function as a deterrent) but women were not permitted to watch.

At the noon eight bells the foreman would take observations to calculate the ship's position, and shortly after that came the highlight of the day – dinner and

the first serving of alcohol. The diet was not very varied but quite substantial and provided enough calories
for the physical work the men had to undertake. A
typical menu would be a pound of biscuit with two
pounds of beef, or a pound of biscuit, a pound of
pork, half a pint of peas and four ounces of cheese. At
the beginning of a voyage fresh meat was generally
available but later it would be salt meat. In port, fresh
vegetables would be obtained if possible. The food
was generally reasonable but unexpectedly long voyages or wartime conditions could affect quality and
leave rations in short supply. Cheese and butter
caused the most complaints since they were the most
difficult commodities to store in an age without re-
frigeration. If a ship was bound for a hot climate, oil
rather than butter was supplied. Although ships carried a lot of water, this was used for cooking and
washing and the men drank beer. Tales of drunken
sailors are, of course, well known. The ration was a
gallon per man per day and, if it was not available,
then grog would be served. Grog was watered down
spirits, usually made with rum, brandy or sometimes
wine, with lemon juice added against scurvy. A pint
of grog would be served with both dinner and supper.
The younger boys would be given half rations and
paid for the other half. The officers would drink just
as much as the men, if not more, since they also
brought their own supplies. Drunkenness was a

perennial problem and the most likely cause of punishment.

The afternoon was spent much as the morning until four o'clock when the hands would be piped to supper. This consisted of something like ship's biscuits and cheese, with more beer or grog. Shortly after the drummer marine would signal the beat to quarters. All men would proceed to the stations that they would be in during a battle. The captain and officers would then inspect the men before the hammocks were piped down from the deck. At eight o'clock in the evening the first watch would be called on deck while the others would sleep until shortly before midnight.

During an engagement all hands would be called and ordered to clear the decks and go to battle stations. The officers' cabins disappeared with all furniture and the bulkheads were removed to the hold. The decks would be wetted and covered with sand as a protection against fire. Damp cloth was placed around all hatches and the magazine room. The boys or those assigned as 'powder monkeys' would collect powder and cartridges from the gunner and all galley fires and lamps were put out. If it was a fleet action, then the captain and the first lieutenant would be on the quarterdeck paying close attention to signals from the admiral. These would have been the procedures taking place in preparation for the battle of Trafalgar.

Trafalgar

Commanding the Mediterranean

Nelson was now in command of the Mediterranean which had always been one of his ambitions. Power in the Mediterranean had been at the heart of the return to hostilities. The French annexations of Leghorn and Elba, and their attempts to expand their trading routes by negotiating with the Barbary States, had alarmed the British Government. However, what really brought the British into war was France's ambition to possess Malta. If the British had lost control of the island their influence, trading and strategic power in the Mediterranean would have collapsed. They were not prepared to surrender Malta for the sake of peace.

Nelson's orders were to defend Malta, Gibraltar and the Kingdom of the Two Sicilies but, most importantly, to observe the French fleet in Toulon and to destroy it if it came out of port. This was crucial because the British needed to prevent it from combining forces with the French fleet at Brest, since Napoleon's army was waiting in Boulogne, ready to invade as soon as the

French navy took control of the Channel. Nelson himself stopped at Gibraltar so that he could assess the
Spanish activity in Cadiz before moving on to Malta. It
was necessary to keep an eye on the Spanish fleet in
case it came out in support of France again or tried to
enter French ports, although he was under orders not
to attack the Spanish unless they broke their neutrality.
His scope for action was limited by the ships and the
manpower at his disposal. His command was about the
same size as France's fleet in Toulon, so he had no real
possibility of countering a combined French-Spanish
attack nor did he have many opportunities of deploy-
ing ships to the vulnerable areas. Neither was there any
chance of reinforcements. Because of these disadvan-
tages, Nelson needed to gather as much intelligence
about the intentions and strategy of the French as he
could so that he could deploy his resources as effi-
ciently as possible. At the beginning of the campaign
there was a lucky break, when Captain Layman captured a small French warship carrying a signal code
book, charts and information about the French Fleet at
St Domingo (modern day Haiti). Subsequent captures
would update and add to this information.

For the majority of the time Nelson kept the fleet
together in blockading Toulon. They were stationed
approximately forty miles away with cruisers providing them with crucial information. There was no point
them being any closer because the French could mon-

itor the British fleet from the hills around Toulon. Being so far out at sea, of course, the British ran the risk that the French could escape from the port. Nelson's strategy to balance this possibility, knowing that there were no targets closer than Malta or Sicily, was to spend his time gathering as much data and knowledge as he could about the local weather patterns, confident that he could exploit this information to determine the potential destinations of the enemy fleet. On board *Victory* Nelson had the services of Reverend Alexander Scott, his chaplain, who was also an experienced intelligence officer and a very competent linguist, capable of translating seized enemy material in French, Spanish and Italian and dealing with foreign correspondence.

Nelson settled back into his command and routine at sea and even came to terms with his separation from Emma. He was certainly more emotionally stable than he had been for some time, even discouraging Emma from a proposed visit and suggesting instead that she turn her attentions to Horatia. Now that Horatia was a little older, Nelson began to write to her directly, sending her a lock of his hair and money to buy a locket. He also arranged to send £4,000, the interest from which was to pay for her education and care. The period of relative calm was broken when Horatia contracted smallpox at the beginning of 1804. Emma had neglected to have her inoculated although

Nelson had been in favour of this. Emma herself was in the late stages of another pregnancy, and he was desperate for news, writing:

'I have my dearest beloved Emma, been so uneasy for this last month; desiring most ardently to hear of your well doing! Captain Capel brought me your letters, sent by Thisbe, from Gibraltar. I opened – opened – found none but December, and early in January. I was in such an agitation! At last, I found one without a date: which, thank God! told my poor heart that you was recovering: but that dear little Emma was no more! and, that Horatia had been so very ill – it altogether upset me. But it was just at bed-time and I had time to reflect, and be thankful to God for sparing you and our dear Horatia. I am sure the loss of one – much more both – would have drove me mad. I was so agitated, as it was, that I was glad it was night, and that I could be by myself. Kiss dear Horatia for me: and tell her to be a dutiful and good child; and, if she is, that we shall always love her.'

Chasing the French

Nelson's own health also began to fail him again, partly due to the fact that he was forever out on deck without taking the trouble to protect himself and partly due to stress. He was particularly concerned about his eyes, noticing that his sight was becoming worse every month. He had improved by June but later in the year, as winter was approaching, he requested leave, hoping to be able to spend Christmas at Merton. It was impossible. The Spanish, as had long been feared, entered the war in December 1804 and a French squadron in Roquefort escaped from the port. These difficulties were compounded in January 1805 when the entire French fleet escaped from Toulon on a particularly stormy night. It was feared that the French were setting in motion their plans to invade Britain. Now, just as before the Battle of the Nile, Nelson was on the hunt for the French fleet, flying along to Naples, Palermo, Malta and Alexandria. In Malta he found out that the storms which had caused the temporary break up of the British blockade had also forced the French back into port almost immediately. On 30 March 1805 Nelson, while he was near Majorca, learnt that the French had sailed again – and again he did not know their whereabouts. By 18 April, he discovered that they had sailed through the Straits of Gibraltar some ten days before, but disadvantageous wind direction prevented the British from following them for almost a month. At the beginning of May more intelligence informed him that the French had picked up Spanish reinforcements from Cadiz and had been sighted sailing for the West Indies. Nelson was 31 days behind the French fleet. By 4 June he reached Barbados where General Robert Brereton, the commander of St Lucia, told him that a fleet of 28 vessels had been seen heading south. Unfortunately, Brereton was wrong. The enemy had gone past Dominica and Antigua to the North and had seized a convoy of valuable British sugar ships. Nelson realised that they must be heading back to Europe and again started to chase, sending a frigate ahead to warn the British.

It must have been an enormously frustrating month, with Nelson desperately disappointed that he had failed to engage the enemy in the West Indies. He still had not sighted them by 18 July. He came together with Collingwood's fleet stationed off Cadiz and stopped at Gibraltar, the first time that he had put his foot on solid ground for nearly two years. On 22 July, off Cape Finisterre, Sir John Calder's squadron had encountered the combined enemy fleet but fought an inconclusive battle, after which the enemy had first put in at Vigo and then gone on in to Ferrol further north, before moving back south to Cadiz. It was not an ideal outcome but it had prevented Napoleon from being able to combine the Franco-Spanish fleet with the Brest fleet and thus take control of the Channel. The fact that Nelson was chasing them was intimidating to the French. Admiral Villeneuve, in charge of the enemy fleet, said that, 'I should be sorry to meet twenty of them. Our naval tactics are antiquated. We know nothing but how to place ourselves in line, and that is just what the enemy wants.' However, the threat of invasion was by no means over. Napoleon still had his army camped in readiness along the French coast and the enemy's combined fleet was still at large.

At Gibraltar Nelson was finally granted leave, reaching Merton on 22 August, still drawing the crowds wherever he went. A witness recorded that, 'Lord Nelson cannot appear in the streets without immediately collecting a retinue, which augments as he proceeds, and when he enters a shop the door is thronged until he comes out, when the air rings with huzzas, and the dark cloud of the populace again moves on, and hangs upon his skirts.' A dinner that Nelson and Emma attended in September provided an interesting insight into Nelson's thoughts on his fame and his awareness of his own vanity. One of the guests was Lady Bessborough, sister to Georgiana, Duchess of Devonshire, and she wrote:

'So far from appearing vain and full of himself, as one had always heard, he was perfectly unassuming and natural. Talking of Popular Applause and his having been Mobbed and Huzzaed in the city, Lady Hamilton wanted to give an account of it, but he stopped her. "Why," said she, "you like to be applauded – you cannot deny it." "I own it," he answered; "popular applause is very acceptable and grateful to me, but no Man ought to be too much elated by it; it is too precarious to be depended upon, and it may be my turn to feel the tide set as strong against me as ever it did for me...Whilst I live I shall do what I think right and best; the country has a right to that from me, but every Man is liable to err in judgement".'

At Merton, Emma had invited as many of his relatives who wanted to come and who could fit into the house. Horatia was there too, now four and a half, but, despite Nelson's wish that she should be there permanently, she had only been sent for on the news of his impending return. Emma was unwilling for her busy social life to be disrupted by a child. She dined out regularly and she was still performing her 'attitudes' to much appreciation, despite having become enormously fat over the years. As ever Nelson was delighted with domesticity at Merton, although he was also dividing his time between his home and professional matters in London, discussing the British position and strategy for combating the French with colleagues at the Admiralty, and with Prime Minister Pitt and the government. He also had his only meeting with Wellington – General Sir Arthur Wellesley, as he then was. At first, Nelson talked rather vainly about himself but, when he realised to whom he was speaking, he switched quickly to what Wellesley considered to be one of the most interesting conversations that he had ever had about war, politics and strategy. Nelson also made a trip to the Admiralty, specifically to arrange for Sir Home Popham's new edition of his signal code to be distributed to the fleet. It was a code that Popham had developed a few years earlier and it was an important tool in improving communication between ships, because it allowed the transmission of specific information rather than the set phrases that had been used previously. Nelson personally took fifty copies with him.

Friday 13 September 1805 was his last day at Merton which he and Emma spent quietly having dinner with friends before Nelson was to leave for Portsmouth later that night. Emma was distraught at the thought of his departure, and one of their guests Lord Minto commented that, 'She tells me that nothing can be more pure and ardent than his flame. He is in many points really a great man, in others a baby.' It seems an apt summary of the contradictions in his character.

Awaiting the Battle

On 14 September Nelson boarded *Victory*. He was rowed out to the ship from one of the bathing machines on the beach to avoid the crowds that had gathered but, nevertheless, he was waved off by hundreds of people. *Victory* sailed for Cadiz where the Franco-Spanish combined fleet was still sheltering. Nelson took over command of the twenty-two ship strong force blockading Cadiz from his friend and second-in-command Cuthbert Collingwood. He was gratified by

the welcome that he received from his officers, saying
that his reception 'on joining the fleet caused the
sweetest sensation in life'. He explained the tactics that
he intended to use. Basically, he planned to attack the
ships in the centre and at the rear of the enemy line
with the intention of disabling them before the leading
ships could turn and come to their support. The aim
was to split his fleet into three divisions, two of which
would sail in parallel lines and cut the enemy line at
right angles at each end. The other division would be
held in reserve to attack the enemy van if it turned to
enter the battle. They would be joined by any of the
other British vessels if they had not suffered too much
damage to support them. A recent discovery shows
that Nelson had been honing his plan for some time. In
2001, as part of the Nelson Letters Project, a quick
sketch was found on the back of some notes he had
made for a meeting in London while on leave which
showed the strategy that he intended to use. His fore-
sight in planning was one of Nelson's greatest strengths
and his success, as Collingwood noted, was 'the effect
of system and nice combination, not of chance'.

Nelson wrote to Emma to tell her the response that
he had had from his captains after outlining his battle
strategy: 'When I came to explain to them the "Nelson
Touch" it was like an electric shock. Some shed tears,
all approved – "It was new – it was singular – it was
simple!" and, from the admirals downwards, it was re-

peated – "It must succeed, if they ever allow us to get at them! You are, my Lord, surrounded by friends whom you inspire with confidence." Some may be Judases, but the majority are certainly much pleased with my commanding them.'

It is not true that Nelson's tactics were completely new and revolutionary – the different elements had mostly been tried before. Nelson was famous for 'breaking the line' but, although, perhaps, he used it to best effect, he had not been the first to do it. New research has also shown that Villeneuve predicted fairly accurately how Nelson would manage the battle of Trafalgar before it started. As Collingwood pointed out, the brilliance and the newness of Nelson's strategy lay in the 'nice combination'.

For now it was a waiting game, as the British fleet waited impatiently for the French to leave port. The fleet was increased to 27 ships of the line over the three weeks leading up to the battle, and on 14 October the French had moved closer to the mouth of the harbour. As Nelson realised the battle was imminent, he wrote to Emma on 19 October: 'My dearest, beloved Emma, the dear friend of my bosom, the signal has been made that the enemy's combined fleet are coming out of port. We have very little wind, so that I have no hopes of seeing them before tomorrow. May the God of Battles crown my endeavours with success; at all events, I will take care that my name shall ever be most dear to you and Horatia, both of whom I love as much as my own life; and as my last writing before the battle will be to you, so I hope in God that I shall live to finish my letter after the Battle. May heaven bless you prays your Nelson & Bronte.

Octr 20 in the morning we were close to the mouth of the Streights, but the wind had not come far enough to the westward to allow the combined fleets to weather the shoals of Trafalgar, but they were counted as far as forty sail of ships of war, which I suppose to be 34 of the line and six frigates. A group of them was seen off the lighthouse off Cadiz this morning, but it blows so very fresh & thick weather that I rather believe they will go into the bay before night...'

Villeneuve had been trying to get his fleet into a regular line of 20 ships, which he believed was the same level of force that Nelson had under his command. His remaining ships he wanted to keep in reserve with Captain Gravina, to support the line where Nelson attacked it. Nelson was heard to comment that 'the 21st will be our day', saying that it was a festival in the Nelson family. It was the day of the annual Burnham Thorpe fair, but also the anniversary of the day when his Uncle Maurice, in command of the *Dreadnought*, had contributed to the defeat of a French squadron during the Seven Years War.

At sunrise on the morning of 21 October,

Villeneuve was utterly dismayed to find that Nelson had five more battleships at his disposal than he had expected. Villeneuve was sailing south-east, following the curve of the coastline, so Nelson turned north-east, thus closing the distance between the fleets down to ten miles. Nelson went to his great cabin to write a codicil to his will, which spoke of Lady Hamilton's service to the country. He wanted to be certain that she and Horatia would be provided for. 'These are the only favours I ask of the King and country,' he wrote, 'at this moment, when I am going to fight their battle. May God bless my King and country and all those I hold dear.'

Over the next couple of hours the British ships gradually came into line, forming two columns. (Facing 33 enemy vessels, there were not enough of them to divide into three.) One was led by Nelson in the *Victory* and the other by Collingwood in the *Royal Sovereign*. Villeneuve reversed course, further closing down the gap between the two fleets. The British went at full sail towards them and the French had just enough sail to maintain their position. They were awaiting battle.

The decks were cleared and ready for action and, as the British advanced, the seamen boosted morale by singing songs such as *Rule Britannia* and *Hearts of Oak*. The furniture from Nelson's cabin was stowed away but he went back and knelt at his desk to write:

'May the Great God, whom I worship, grant to my Country, and for the benefit of Europe in general, a great and glorious victory; and may no misconduct in anyone tarnish it; and may humanity after Victory be the predominant feature in the British fleet. For myself, individually, I commit my life to Him who made me, and may the blessing light upon my endeavours for serving my Country faithfully. To Him I resign myself and the just cause which is entrusted to me to defend. Amen. Amen. Amen.'

Returning to the deck he sent out the famous signal to the fleet, 'England confides that every man will do his duty.' As time was pressing, the word 'confides' was not spelt out, because it needed a flag for each letter, but instead 'expects' was used, since there was a single flag to represent that word. The essence of the message was that Nelson knew that everyone would do their utmost and it was greeted with cheers around the fleet. Nelson only sent two more signals, 'Prepare to anchor' and 'Engage the enemy more closely'.

Opening Fire

The enemy line began to fire at midday when Nelson's ships were about a mile away from them. The British fleet went head on into the broadsides of the combined Spanish and French fleet. Nelson's own aim was Villeneuve's flagship. There was some concern from his officers that the visible decorations on Nelson's uniform would make him vulnerable to sniper fire. Some have later claimed that he persisted in wearing it as a matter of vanity but it is unlikely that he had another and he would certainly have considered it dishonourable to hide himself in the face of the enemy. He also balked at the suggestion of moving into a different ship. Nelson was not a man to remove himself from action and he always fought alongside his men. It is not that he wanted to die. He had too much at home to which he wanted to return. He had always been prepared to die for his country but this was not the same as having a death wish.

The *Royal Sovereign* was the first to be hit, but soon retaliated by bringing down the top gallant yard of the enemy vessel. Next it was the turn of *Victory* to come under fire. The first two shots fell into the water and the third whistled through the sails. Seven or eight enemy ships were concentrating their fire on the *Victory* and the wheel was smashed. The ship then had to be steered manually with around 40 men needed to turn the tiller. *Victory* had been sailing as if she intended to attack the leading ships of the enemy line but now turned to attack those in the centre, choosing the 80 gun *Bucentaure*, Villeneuve's flagship. The firing on both sides was ferocious, and the French ships moved closer together. Captain Hardy later remarked that they 'closed like a forest'. The attempt to cut the enemy line had left *Victory* trapped and fighting on three sides. *Victory* crashed into the *Redoutable*, with the yard arm of *Victory* becoming entangled in the French ship's rigging and immobilising the British ship. However, *Bucentaure* was so ravaged by British fire that Villeneuve was stranded, unable to fire or signal or make an escape. British gunnery was second to none and the speed of the gunners reportedly superior to that of the French and Spanish, which was certainly a factor in the outcome.

Above the main yards of the *Redoutable* stood snipers on a platform aiming at the officers on *Victory's* quarterdeck. Just after one o'clock Hardy realised that Nelson was no longer by his side. He saw him down on his knees, fingertips supporting him on the deck before his arm gave way and he fell. A musket shot had entered his left shoulder, punctured his left lung, cut an artery, shattered his spine and lodged itself just under his right shoulder. He was carried down to the orlop deck for medical attention where the surgeon, William Beatty, was busy with mounting casualties. On his way down Nelson was still giving orders to adjust the tiller ropes. He also covered his face so that he was hidden from the crew and, therefore, their morale would not be affected by news of his injuries.

Above, the engagement with *Redoutable* was coming to a close. The French had tried to board but were continually held back by the heavy fire and they finally surrendered when the British *Temeraire*'s carronades blasted through her. There was no longer a threat to the *Victory*.

The Death of Nelson

Nelson, realising that his death was imminent, anxiously repeated to the chaplain: 'Remember me to Lady Hamilton! remember me to Horatia! remember me to all my friends. Doctor, remember me to Mr Rose [a friend of Prime Minister Pitt]: tell him I have made a will, and left Lady Hamilton and Horatia to my country.' Nelson began to lose any feeling below his chest but he was in severe pain and having difficulty breathing as his blood flowed into his left lung at every heartbeat. His thoughts alternated between his personal life and the battle in hand, but he still had time for others. When a midshipman, who was the son of a colleague from the Nicaraguan campaign, came down, he begged to be remembered to his father. He was also comforted by the cheers that went up from the crew every time another enemy ship surrendered. Captain Hardy came down to see him at about 2.30 because Nelson wanted to question him about the battle and he told him that 12 or 14 vessels had struck and that no British vessels had surrendered. Nelson told Hardy that he wanted Emma to have his hair and his personal belongings. Beatty then attended to Nelson and, on

being told that his wound was fatal as he already believed, the admiral uttered the famous line 'God be
praised, I have done my duty'. Hardy returned at
around 3.30 to declare a glorious victory. Nelson reminded him to anchor and that he did not want his
body to be thrown overboard, and pleaded with him
to take care of Emma. With Emma on his mind he
asked Hardy to kiss him. (The idea that he said
'kismet,' the Turkish for 'fate' was a Victorian inven-
tion at a time when the idea of two men kissing was
not considered seemly for a hero.) Hardy kissed him
on the cheek after which Nelson said, 'Now I am satisfied,' and repeated his line, 'Thank God I have done
my duty.' Hardy, clearly moved, bent down again to
kiss him on the forehead but Nelson was losing consciousness and had to ask who it was. 'God bless you
Hardy', he said when he learnt. Hardy returned to the
deck in his grief. To make the admiral more comfortable his steward turned him on to his side, although
this hastened death as blood began to drain from the
left lung to his right. Nelson turned to the chaplain
saying, 'Doctor, I have *not* been a *great* sinner,' and his
words became less coherent as his breathing began to
fail. The chaplain and his steward continued to rub his
chest which brought some relief from the pain. He
kept repeating 'Thank God I have done my duty', his
last coherent line. Nelson died at 4.30 just as the fighting was coming to a close.

Nineteen enemy vessels had been taken and one was on fire. 449 British had been killed and 1,214 wounded though this was low in comparison to the 6,000 enemy casualties. There were also 2,000 prisoners taken. Many lives were lost in the storm that raged after the battle, giving the men little respite while they tried to repair rigging and secure the prize ships, many of which were to be taken by the storm. As the news of Nelson's death became known through the fleet, men were weeping openly. One wrote home that, 'I hope it is not injustice to the Second in Command...who fought like a hero, to say that the Fleet under any other, never would have performed what they did under Lord N. But under Lord N it seemed like inspiration to most of them.'

The loss of Nelson almost overshadowed the victory itself. Beatty put the Admiral's body in a cask filled with brandy which was replaced with wine when the *Victory* put in for repairs at Gibraltar. Legend has it that the brandy was drunk by the seamen. For the rest of the journey home Nelson thus travelled in the barrel which was secured to the mizzen mast in his great cabin, and guarded by a sentry at all times.

After Trafalgar

The Funeral

Back in Britain any joy over the victory at Trafalgar was also silenced by Nelson's death. A National Thanksgiving day was arranged for 5 December and over a million pounds was donated to the wounded and to families of the bereaved.

On 23 December a yacht met *Victory* close to the Nore to carry the coffin up the Thames to Greenwich. Along the whole route, ships lowered their flags to half mast, bells tolled and guns were fired at Tilbury and Gravesend. The coffin was placed in the Painted Hall at Greenwich Hospital where it is believed that up to 100,000 people filed past the body.

On 7 January 1806 a group of seamen chosen from *Victory* arrived to join a procession with barges and boats that stretched for two miles along the river and proceeded to Whitehall where Nelson was taken to the Admiralty. The state funeral was to take place on 9 January and that morning the procession assembled in Hyde Park with entry by ticket only. It included light dragoons, infantry, cavalry, artillery and grenadiers, followed by the crew of the *Victory* and pensioners from Greenwich hospital. Naval officers and dignitaries followed with the Prince of Wales at the back of the procession closest to the coffin. The funeral carriage was shaped like *Victory* with a bow and stern and drawn by six black horses. Along the route to St Paul's Cathedral, where the funeral would take place, were crowds of people, who made almost no sound, simply removing their hats as the coffin passed. The crowds were so large that soldiers lined the route to keep control.

The service lasted for almost five hours and the coffin was lowered into the crypt beneath the dome in a sarcophagus once intended for Cardinal Wolsey. Nelson was the first commoner who had warranted such a monument. The only disturbance to the solemn proceedings came from the seamen who tore off parts of *Victory*'s ensign to keep as reminders. The funeral cost £14,000 and was the most extravagant and spectacular that London had ever seen. In terms of its impact, as Andrew Lambert notes in his recent book on Nelson, it has probably only been matched by those of Churchill and Lady Diana.

Nelson's Legacy

Nelson would have been devastated that Emma was not invited to the funeral. She took to her bed in desperate grief, scribbling on the last of his letters to her 'Oh miserable, wretched Emma. Oh glorious and happy Nelson.' Nelson's last wish that she and Horatia should receive a legacy was never granted. Pitt, who had intended to act upon Nelson's request died, before he was able to do anything about it, and his successor, Grenville, was not one of Emma's admirers. Nelson's brother William had been made an earl, with a considerable pension of £6,000 and another £100,000 to buy a house, but he was also unwilling to help her. She was not legally entitled to any state provision and, although many of his friends petitioned on her behalf, nothing was to come of it. In 1814, she was in prison for debt, having spent everything that Nelson had left her and sold both Merton and Nelson's letters. Nelson's friends bailed her out but she died penniless in Calais the following January. Horatia fared better, although she had no help from the state either. She was taken in by her Matcham relatives and grew up to become the wife of a country parson. Emma never acknowledged that she was her mother. Slight amends were made in 1854 after a Victorian biographer of Nelson, Thomas Pettigrew, raised the issue of Horatia's paternity and Nelson's dying wish. After protracted negotiations, a civil pension of £300 was raised to be shared between Horatia's three daughters.

Following his death, the outpouring of Nelson tributes, paintings and biographies was immediate, as was confirmation of his status as a national hero, almost a god. He was an important symbol in uniting Britain and providing a focus of national identity in the ten years before Napoleon was finally defeated at Waterloo. He was the inspiration for artists and writers alike, most notably Turner and Coleridge, but also for popular theatre and songs. Memorials sprung up across the major cities in the country as well as in places as far away as Bridgetown, Barbados. London, however, was a little slow to follow suit. Although the idea had been discussed in Parliament as early as 1816 and Trafalgar Square had been named in 1835, Nelson's Column was not finished until 1843. It was designed by William Railton and it took three years to construct the 185-feet-high granite column and the 18-feet-tall Nelson. Landseer's bronze lions at the base were not added for another 24 years. The report in the *London Illustrated News* in October 1843 shows the feeling that the statue was long over due:

'The statue of Nelson – the hero of Trafalgar – having been completed, has been for a short space made visible to the public from a nearer point of view than many of them are destined to have of it in future. It has been exhibited on the surface of terra firma, previous to its elevation to the summit of the column, henceforth Nelson's Column, in Trafalgar Square – a locality which, were it not for the common-place character of the front of the National Gallery would become the finest open space in the metropolis...Those who have seen his "Nelson" – colossal in size – the features true to nature-a portrait in stone, not an idealism of a hero-the costume, that of an English Admiral, a costume which no skill can elevate to dignity, or transform to the graceful-will have received, probably, a mingled impression. Unless they remembered they were looking at an object intended to be seen only at a great elevation, they may have been surprised at a sort of coarseness in the workmanship. Yet it has all the finish that can be required, and it has the great merit of likeness and character-one perhaps inseparable from the other in the countenance of such a man as Nelson. It has the sharp, angular features, the expression of great activity of mind, but of little mental grandeur; of quickness of perception and decision; and withal, that sad air, so perceptible in the best portraits of the warrior, of long-continued physical pain and suffering, the consequence of his many wounds, which accompanied him throughout his brightest triumphs, though it never abated his ardour or weakened his energies. The expression is a peculiar one; it is more afflicting to the eye than the expression of deep thought, and though as mournful, it is less abstracted than that of meditation. If ever man earned his greatness, both by action and suffering, it was the hero of Trafalgar. While we feel a satisfaction that a public memorial to him is now completed, we cannot help regretting that more than thirty years should have elapsed before so obvious a duty to his renown was accomplished. His monument can hardly be considered as a national tribute to his fame: it is a funeral record, it is raised in a sacred spot, and is consecrated by religion; the interest it possesses is of a higher and more sacred kind. This statue is the public and secular memorial – the tribute of the citizen to the warrior – and till now, in the metropolis of the nation he fought and died for, that tribute has remained unpaid!.. The statue was thrown open to the public last Friday and Saturday, October 27 and 28, and was visited by a hundred thousand persons.'

Monuments to Nelson have continued to have political resonance up to our own times. Nelson's Pillar, which stood in O'Connell Street, Dublin and was erected in 1808, was destroyed by an IRA bomb in 1966. There are questions over retaining the monument in Barbados, with its references to the colonial past. Hitler considered Nelson's Column as the 'symbol of British naval might and world domination'. Had he succeeded in invading Britain in the Second World War, he planned to relocate it to Berlin.

Nelson in the 20th and 21st Centuries

Over the late Victorian period interest in Nelson waned as Britain entered a period of peace, although at the end of the century there was a revived interest in the Navy and a new biography was published after a 30-year gap. Nelson scholarship received a boost in the 1930s with the development of the National Maritime Museum, which brought together many Nelson artefacts and documents and made him central to the collections. The *Victory* too was restored although it had remained a shrine since 1805. Even today the ship is still in commission as the base for the Second Sea Lord.

During the Second World War Nelson's image was invoked as an inspiration to the Navy and, for propaganda purposes, as a symbol of national identity. The actor Leslie Howard, who had had success in Hollywood, returned to Britain to aid the war effort and played the part of Nelson in a pageant. On the steps of St Paul's Cathedral, he recited Nelson's last prayer before the Battle of Trafalgar. A journalist reported that 'I shall never forget the electric thrill that ran through the crowd when he appeared. That brief moment stole the show'. Nelson was inevitably mentioned in almost every publication on the navy published throughout the war. *The Royal Navy at War*, published in 1941 by John Murray with photographs from the Ministry of Information, included a typical eulogy:

'The memory of Nelson remains immortal, because besides being the most successful naval leader in our history, he never failed to interest himself in the welfare of the British seaman, and he invariably showed kindness and consideration to all those under his command.'

This aspect of his character – his interest in the ordinary seaman – was particularly emphasised during the Second World War because it fitted in with the concept of 'the People's War'. It reflected changing attitudes towards class, and the ways in which history was no longer focussed exclusively on the nobility, the government and royalty but was beginning to include ordinary working people. Nelson, with his unremarkable background and his titles earned through merit rather than birth, suited this mood. Churchill was also a great Nelson fan, and his favourite film was Alexander Korda's *Lady Hamilton*, made in 1941, which he watched repeatedly.

At the end of the war when the focus of the country was firmly on the future, Nelson's importance in defining national identity declined, although scholarly interest in him continued, particularly in his private life which had been for so long underplayed. In recent decades, he has continued to feature in popular culture and there has been a steady stream of books, films and plays about him. Terence Rattigan's play *Bequest to a Nation*, written in 1966, was televised in that same year, and filmed in 1973 with Peter Finch as Nelson and Glenda Jackson as Emma, *I Remember Nelson:*

Recollections of a Hero's Life, was a 1982 television series and the novel by Barry Unsworth, *Losing Nelson*, was published to great acclaim in 1999. These are just a few examples. There has also been a surge in popular interest in the age of sail in general as the success of Patrick O'Brian's naval novels, the film of *Master and Commander* that was based on them and the television series based on C. S. Forester's *Hornblower* books, shows.

The bicentenary of Trafalgar in 2005 has thrust Nelson back into the national consciousness and provided the impetus for a fresh look at his life and renewed academic research. He still symbolises many of the values that are relevant to Britain in the 21st century – the refusal to accept tyranny and the determination to succeed against all the odds. However, it is not just these lofty aspirations that make him stand the test of time as a part of British national identity. There is also the human side of his character – his great passion, his impetuousness, his vanity and his kindness. It is these qualities that have been the focus of recent interest in him as much as his prowess in the arena of war – a reflection of the complexity of the man still held to be the greatest naval leader of all time.

Timeline of Nelson's Life

1758
29th September, Nelson is born to Edmund and Catherine Nelson at Burnham Thorpe, Norfolk.

1767
His mother dies.

1771
At 12 years old joins the Royal Navy on the *Raisonnable* rated as a midshipman.

1773
Joins the Arctic expedition on *Carcass*.
Joins *Seahorse* for the East Indies.

1777
Passes the examination for lieutenant.
Appointed to *Lowestoft*.

1778

Appointed to 1st lieutenant on the *Bristol*, then commander of *Badger*.

1781

Nelson is appointed Captain of the *Albemarle*.

1785

Meets Frances Nisbet on Nevis.

1787

Marries Frances Nisbet and returns to England.

1788

Settles down to life with Fanny back in Burnham Thorpe.

1793

First meets Lady Hamilton in Naples.

1794

Loses the sight in his right eye at Calvi, Corsica.

1797

Battle of Cape St Vincent. Promoted to Rear Admiral. Loses his right arm at Santa Cruz, Tenerife.

1798

Battle of the Nile. Created Baron Nelson. Evacuates the Sicilian Royal Family and the Hamiltons from Naples to Palermo.

1799

Made Duke of Bronte, Sicily.

1800

Returns to England with the Hamiltons.

1801

Promoted to vice-admiral. Birth of Horatia. Battle of Copenhagen. Created Viscount Nelson. Buys Merton Place.

1803

Sir William Hamilton dies. Appointed Commander-in-Chief in the Mediterranean.

1805

21st October Battle of Trafalgar. Nelson dies in battle, aged 47.

1806

State funeral in St Paul's Cathedral.

Further Reading

Clarke & M'Arthur: *The Life of Admiral Nelson 2 vols.* London: 1809.

One of the first biographies of Nelson responsible for many of the persitent myths

Hibbert, Christopher. *Nelson: A Personal History.* London: Viking, 1994.

A very readable account with many anecdotes.

Knight, Roger. *The Pursuit of Victory.* London: Allen Lane, 2005.

A really comprehensive biography of Nelson, which goes back and looks at all the original sources.

Lambert, Andrew. *Nelson: Brittania's God of War.* London: Faber, 2004.

Excellent read which concentrates on Nelson's naval, rather than personal, life.

Morriss, Roger. *Nelson: The Life and Letters of a Hero.* London: Collins & Brown, 1996.

Short readable introduction to Nelson.

O'Brian, Patrick. *Men-of-War: Life in Nelson's Navy.* New York: Norton, 1995.

Slight but useful overview.

Rodger, N.A.M. *The Wooden World: An Anatomy of the Georgian Navy.* London: Fontana, 1986.

The best book available on the working of the Georgian Navy.

Southey, Robert: *Life of Nelson.* London, 1813.

Probably the most influential biography of Nelson available in hundreds of reprints, though it owes much to Clarke & M'Arthur. Southey became poet laureate and one of the book's greatest attractions is that it is beautifully written.

White, Colin (ed). *The Nelson Companion.* London: Alan Sutton, 1995.

This is a useful collection of essays about Nelson covering topics such as portraits, letters and Nelson relics. Colin White is a leading expert on Nelson and in charge of the Nelson's Letters project.

Other Useful Sources and Places to Visit

The National Maritime Museum, Greenwich London: (www.nmm.ac.uk) The museum has a permanent Nelson collection with many Nelson relics including the uniform that he wore at Trafalgar. The archives contain many articles and letters relating to Nelson.

Opposite the National Maritime Museum is the Old Royal Naval College where it is possible to visit The Painted Hall where Nelson laid in state.

Burnham Thorpe, Norfolk. The parsonage no longer exists but the church (All Saints) can still be visited.

Chatham Dockyards, Kent (www.chdt.org.uk) The Georgian dockyard where HMS *Victory* was built has been preserved and is open to the public.

Victory is preserved at the historic dockyard in Portsmouth and can be visited (www.flagship.org.uk)

Societies

The Nelson Society: (www.nelson-society.org.uk)

The 1805 Club: (www.admiralnelson.org) The 1805 Club conserves and maintains monuments and memorials to Nelson and those associated with him, from ordinary seaman to fellow admirals.

The Society for Nautical Research (www.snr.org) General naval history.

Index